SEAGOING KNOTS

OLTRE L'ORIZZONTE

ELBA, SEPT 5

L.O.A. 23 FT
L.W.L. 20 "
BEAM 2.20 M.
DRAUGHT 1.25 "

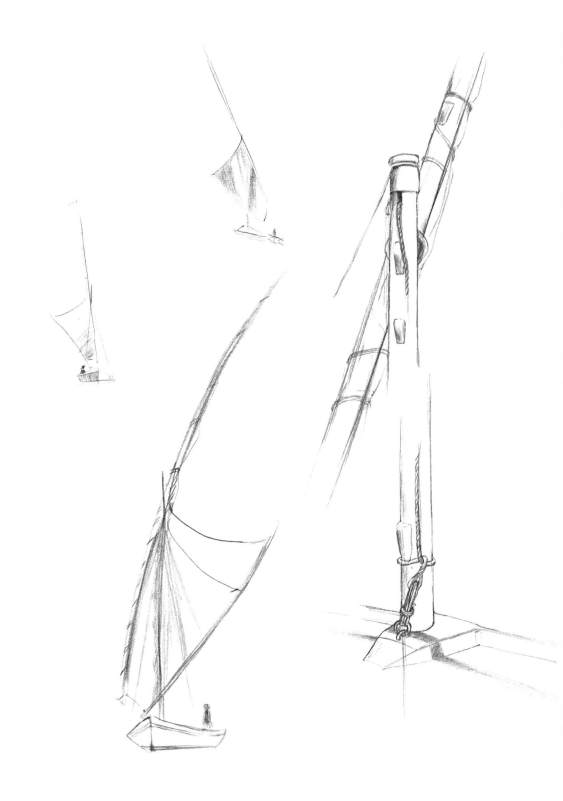

By Frank Rosenow

THE DITTY BAG BOOK

MANUAL ART: A Practical Guide to Drawing and Painting

CANVAS AND ROPECRAFT FOR THE PRACTICAL BOATOWNER

SEAGOING KNOTS

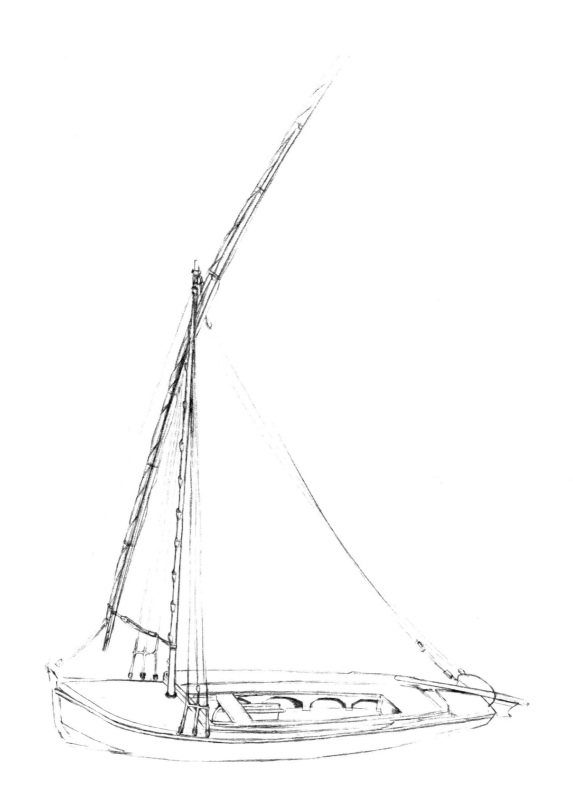

Seagoing
KNOTS

FRANK ROSENOW

W. W. NORTON & COMPANY   New York London

This book is composed in Goudy Old Style. Composition by New England
Typographic Service. Manufacturing by Halliday Lithographers. Book design by
Margaret Wagner.

First Edition
Library of Congress Cataloging-in-Publication Data

Rosenow, Frank, 1944–
    Seagoing knots/Frank Rosenow.
        p.   cm.
    Includes bibliographical references.
    1. Knots and splices. I. Title.
VM533.R67   1990
623.88′82—dc20   89-71040

ISBN 0-393-03338-4

W.W. Norton & Company, Inc., 500 Fifth Avenue, New York, N.Y. 10110
W.W. Norton & Company Ltd., 37 Great Russell Street, London WC1B 3NU

CONTENTS

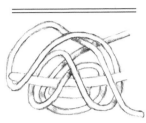

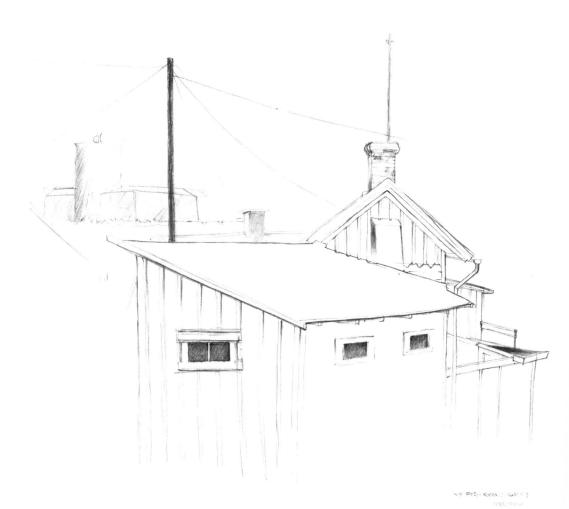

INTRODUCTION

Emil Landell, Master Pilot retired, came down the lane in his dark-blue Sunday best, sober and freshly shaven. The children came the other way, escaping from the small island's church.

"Good day to you, Uncle Emil," we greeted him, bowing smartly.

Brightening under the gilt-edged visor of his master's cap, Uncle Emil pulled out his big leather purse and selected a small silver coin for each of us. To further please him, one of our number said,

"May we look at your knots, Uncle?"

The old pilot glanced only briefly towards the place of worship.

"All right, you scamps," he said.

We trooped after him up a garden walk which was bordered with pink emperor helmet shells from distant shores. Under the gingerbread eaves of his villa, Uncle Emil's study was lined with varnished display boards. On them crowded sisal, hemp, and cotton lines, knotted, spliced and served over in every configuration known to a deep-water sailor with a fair memory of the 19th century. There were bits of rope colored in ochre, straw, and a full chalky white. The servings were tarred over in jet black, or a red as bright as a stick of sealing wax. The room smelt of Stockholm tar mixed with the new-mown scent of sisal fibers.

The boards, brimming with knots that had had their vigor of movement arrested, seemed to the children like a great butterfly collection, pinned down and deprived of life. Taken out of the natural context in which they would be tied, the knots made little sense. So we took our leave and ran off to a nearby pond to catch tadpoles.

Crewing on my grandfather's fishing boat and sailing the family skiff, we did learn the clove hitch, half-hitches and the flip-over bowline knots we could see a reason and use for. Add the square knot and a slipped hitch and you have my knot vocabulary for a great many years at sea.

Nor is this unusual. Dr. David L. Edwards, after taking his 31-foot ketch *Azulão* from Los Angeles to the bay of Naples, recently confided that he had managed it using four knots: The bowline, the clove hitch, the square knot, and the figure eight.

AZULÃO'S
8 FT "COLUMBIA"
SAILING DINGHY

Geoffrey Budworth, during ten years afloat with the River Police in the tidal waters of the Thames in the Port of London, found six knots sufficient for "everything imaginable." They were:

the bowline
the clove hitch
the sheet bend
round turn and two half hitches
the killick hitch
lighterman's back mooring hitch

Of these, the lighterman's back mooring hitch (Ashley knot 1795) is not usually practiced in yachting gauge cordage, and the killick hitch saw its primary use on the Thames in securing decomposing bodies.

The complexity of knots that do exist we owe to the great commercial and naval sailing era that Uncle Emil saw the end of. To him, the knots in his study were not specimens tied to a board but examples of knots which had staved off disaster before an Atlantic gale, and many more such feats.

To respect and remember a knot, you have to experience its worth in service. One of my best-loved knots, the rolling hitch, gained this status by saving *Moth* from being thrown against a harbor wall at Heraklion, Crete. A trabaccoli man took our line at a critical moment and had it secured to a hawser in a twinkle.

To have a knot practically demonstrated is in itself a boon. You can photograph or draw it for someone else's benefit but sleight of hand is best shown and best remembered when passing from one hand to another.

I have been fortunate in learning most of my knots this way, from many hands, and will try to present them in the light they were revealed to me. The knots are not as numerous as those of Uncle Emil, but my aim is to pass on those that have proved themselves in my own seafaring. Of those I can speak (and draw) with conviction.

Like good friends, all these knots have their quirks which one needs to be acquainted with, but which, when applied with due regard to the quirks, are utterly reliable.

I have rejected knots like the carrick bend and the sheepshank, which, though in every book of knots, are unwieldy and rarely of use in recreational sailing.

To show the geometry of a knot, I have drawn it in different stages of being formed. On a page, the sequence is from left to right, usually starting top left. Where a knot is illustrated by a single drawing, it is usually shown very loosely tied, so that the geometry is plain to see. In using them, one must remember that after a knot has been tied it needs to be worked into shape. A lopsided, collapsing knot is ugly and dangerous. Aim for a reasonably tight, symmetrical knot in which the parts are snugly balanced against one another. For instance, a bowline should never be relied upon until fully drawn up and coaxed into balance.

To be able to retain these knots, it helps greatly to have a sweet and pliable line to practice with. I am very fond of a cotton braid which I first came across in Turkish ports but have since seen in Marseilles (sold by the ship chandler in the northeast corner of the old harbor). It is small in dimension—the drawing shows it nearly full size—and lacks a core or has a very soft, straight one. It is handy and ties very well and I have a hunch it is the same "cotton banding" which Ashley (of *Ashley's Book of Knots*, 1944, New York) recommends: "If fifty cents is mailed to Warren Rope, Box 76, Westport Point, Massachusetts, a ball of cotton banding will be mailed to the reader." Unfortunately, this arrangement has long lapsed.

Pick out a knot or two as the spirit moves you and practice those on and off for a few days for every conceivable purpose. That way, the knot will become a friend, loyally waiting to be called upon in port or at sea. The choice of knots for this book has been made with yachting-gauge cordage in mind, ranging from cord to line 20mm in diameter. Had it been written for tugboat hands, a different set of knots would have had to be considered.

Fair winds!

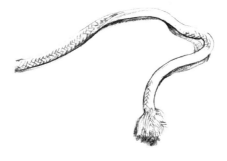

TURKISH CORD

LINES AND LASHINGS

The knot takes its cue from line.

Native people like the Polynesians or Eskimos have lacked access to manufactured line even in recent times and often make do with strips cut from the bark of trees or, in Greenland, with strips cut from seal skins or young walrus hides.

In these "lines" you will find knots a scarce item. Instead, there will be plenty of lashings.

On the island of Huahine, in French Polynesia, all the local produce from live crabs to taro roots is lashed with bark strips. The crab lashing starts with a loop but the trussing up is then effected without any knots at all. Friction and the way the bark fibers deform in the final, acute tuck effects a tenacious hold.

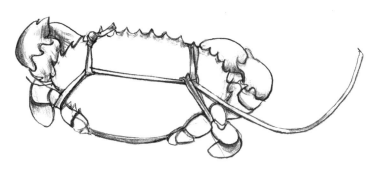

REED STRAIGHTJACKET
FOR LIVE CRABS +
F. POLYNESIA

The tarot bundles, for which broader strips are used, are held together with a simple clove hitch, relying on the still sappy bark strips for holding power.

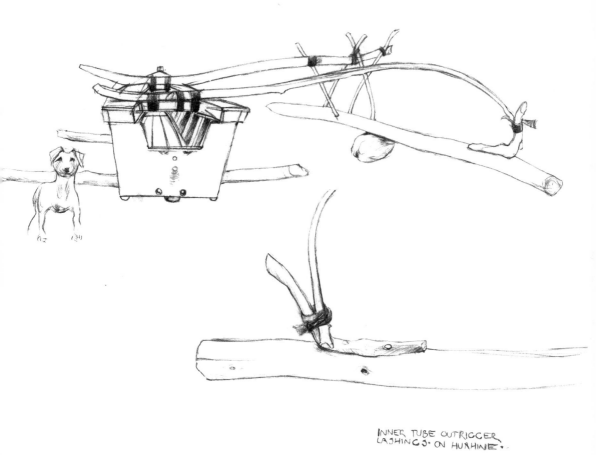

INNER TUBE OUTRIGGER
LASHINGS ON HUAHINE.

On the beaches and coves of the island you find planked outriggers with the cross members attached to hull and float by way of rubber lashings, culled from automotive inner tubes. Friction and stretch do all the work and there is not a knot in sight.

On the Pacific island of Ile des Pins, south of New Caledonia, outriggers are still made from logs with both the main hull and the float hollowed out. Synthetic rope purchased from the stores in Noumea is used for lashings and rigging. Even so, knots are still conspicuously absent.

For instance, to tighten up a shroud, the line is doubled up a couple of times to make a lashing and several frapping turns are taken. Then the simplest of all knots, an overhand, is made on the end which is pushed through between parts of the tensioned lashing to anchor the whole construction.

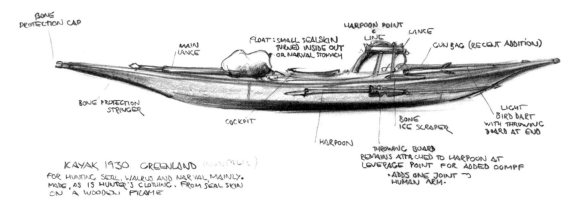

BONE
PROTECTION CAP

MAIN
LANCE

FLOAT: SMALL SEALSKIN
TURNED INSIDE OUT
OR NARVAL STOMACH

HARPOON POINT
&
LINE   LANCE

GUN BAG (RECENT ADDITION)

BONE PROTECTION
STRINGER

COCKPIT

HARPOON

BONE
ICE SCRAPER

LIGHT
BIRD DART
WITH THROWING
BOARD AT END

THROWING BOARD
REMAINS ATTACHED TO HARPOON AT
LEVERAGE POINT FOR ADDED OOMPF
• ADDS ONE JOINT TO
HUMAN ARM.

KAYAK 1930 GREENLAND (QAJAQ)
FOR HUNTING SEAL, WALRUS AND NARVAL MAINLY.
MADE, AS IS HUNTER'S CLOTHING, FROM SEAL SKIN
ON A WOODEN FRAME

NARVAL = NARWHAL

EVERY PIECE OF KAYAK EQUIPMENT HAS ITS PLACE,
USUALLY FOR A GOOD REASON. THE COILED
HARPOON LINE ON THE STAND IN FRONT OF THE
COCKPIT PASSES ON THE RIGHT-HAND SIDE OF
THE HUNTER TO THE FLOAT BEHIND HIM. IT IS
ATTACHED WITH A TOGGLE

THE FLOAT STAYS ON THE BOAT BY HAVING A WOODEN
WEDGE CONNECTION TO THE DECK SECURING
LINES

THE MAIN LANCE IS AFT, TO THE LEFT, LEAVING THE
RIGHT SIDE FREE SO THAT NOTHING OBSTRUCTS
THE FLOAT AS IT IS CAST OFF

THE BIRD DART, ON THE FOREDECK, IS ON THE LEFT
SIDE, PARTICULARLY IF A GUN OR LIGHT LANCE
IS CARRIED AND HAS A GREATER CLAIM TO
ACCESSIBILITY.

TOWING TACKLE, FOR TAKING THE CATCH BACK
WITH THE AID OF A FLOAT, IS AT THE
BOTTOM OF THE KAYAK.

THE HUNTER PADDLES SOFTLY AND, SEEING A SEAL, TRIES TO APPROACH
INTO THE WIND WITH THE SUN BEHIND HIM. THE HARPOON IS NOW
ON THE RIGHT SIDE OF THE FOREDECK, RESTING IN A BONE HOOK
INCORPORATED IN THE LINE CRADLE SUPPORT

CLOSE TO THE SEAL, THE HUNTER WRIGGLES THE KAYAK TO THE LEFT,
GRASPS THE BROAD END OF THE THROWING BOARD, AND THROWS.
GRABBING THE DISENGAGED BOARD WITH HIS TEETH, HE FLINGS THE
FLOAT FAR TO THE RIGHT AND PLACES THE MAIN LANCE ON THE RIGHT
HAND SIDE OF THE FORE DECK, READY TO STAB THE SEAL TO DEATH.

THE DEAD SEAL IS HAULED UP, INFLATED THROUGH THE NOSTRILS, PLUGGED UP
WITH WOODEN PEGS AND TOWED OFF.

IN CALM SEAS WITH FAT SEALS, A RIFLE IS USED AS THERE IS
NO DANGER OF THE SEAL SINKING.

Eskimo knot work, from its high point at the beginning of this century, also displays a partiality to lashings and an even more developed sense of how to use the characteristics of a line. These lines were precision work in themselves, being cut in uniform strips from the skins of young barbed seal or walrus. A soaking in urine gives them the right amount of pliability and stretch.

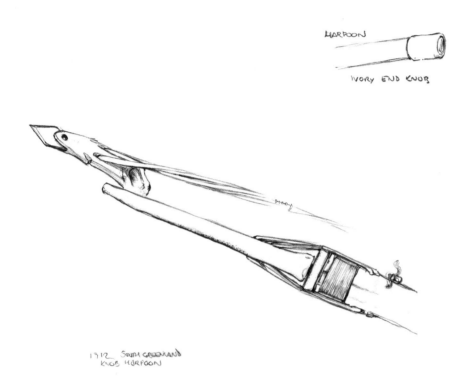

HARPOON

IVORY END KNOB

1912 SOUTH GREENLAND
KNOB HARPOON

In the drawing of a South Greenland kayak from around 1930, the above detail shows the walrus tusk foreshaft of the harpoon. A socket in the foot of it corresponds to a peg in the bone mounting plate of the harpoon. A baleen lashing holds the two together and there are no knots save an overhand at the end. To make the harpoon tip, another bit of walrus tusk is hollowed out to rest on the foreshaft. A tensioned seal thong holds it in place and via the harpoon attaches with a bone toggle to the float. The arrangement will keep a seal struck with the harpoon afloat.

The small lashings are often made using a deer sinew threaded on bird or fish bone needles, resulting in a permanent seizing.

TO AMASS WEALTH BY THE MILLION DOES
NOT COMPARE WITH THE MASTERY OF
A SMALL SKILL

CHINESE PROVERB

EYE PROTECTORS
(DRIFTWOOD)

HARPOON LINE ARRANGEMENT

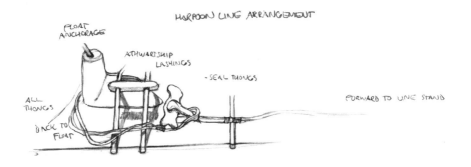

FLOAT
ANCHORAGE

ATHWARTSHIP
LASHINGS

- SEAL THONGS

ALL
THONGS

BACK TO
FLOAT

FORWARD TO LINE STAND

THROWING BOARD

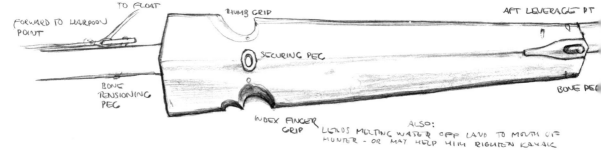

TO FLOAT

THUMB GRIP

AFT LEVERAGE PT

FORWARD TO HARPOON
POINT

SECURING PEG

BONE
TENSIONING
PEG

INDEX FINGER
GRIP

BONE PEG

ALSO:
LEADS MELTING WATER OFF LAND TO MOUTH OF
HUNTER - OR MAY HELP HIM RIGHTEN KAYAK

SPERM-WHALE TUSK
MOUNTING

LOOSE, 18 CM FORESHAFT
OF WALRUS TUSK WITH
SOCKET IN FOOT WHICH
CORRESPONDS TO PEG
IN BONE MOUNTING
PLATE

BALEEN LASHING

HARPOON HEAD OF WALRUSTUSK
WITH BARBS

FLOAT ATTACHED AT
HAVELAND PEAT WOOD
STOPPERS

2.80 METER HARPOON
HUNDE EYLAND

REAR PEG ADJUSTMENTS ACCORDING
TO HOW STRAIGHT IT FLIES
LEFT = CURVE THE PEG

SEAGOING KNOTS

In the south of France, I have several times observed a boat owner tying up his craft by carefully winding the mooring line a dozen times or so around a bollard. However, while lashings teach us about friction in the turns of a line and to appreciate and make use of individual line quality, I do not wish to advocate them for mooring yachts.

Yet, having trained as a sailmaker under the first-class hand seaming man Gunnar Andersson, I cannot foreswear lashings—in the shape of palm-and-needle seizings and whippings—as a most useful and permanent aid to the tying of knots proper. For the material and techniques involved I must direct the reader to another book, *Canvas and Rope Craft*, published also by W. W. Norton, which covers proper hand seaming in depth.

As for lashings, the present-day sailor will want to reduce the twists to a reasonable number and we naturally turn to knots. Modern lines with uniform girth and quality help us tie them securely.

The pliability of a line, its willingness to turn and intertwine to make a secure knot is a hard thing to define but good line will feel handy and vigorous in your hand rather than hard and resisting.

At sea, hemp, manila, and sisal have given way to the synthetic and more durable manmade fibers in polyester (Dacron) and nylon. In plain-laid rope, the configuration has been handed down from natural fiber rope.

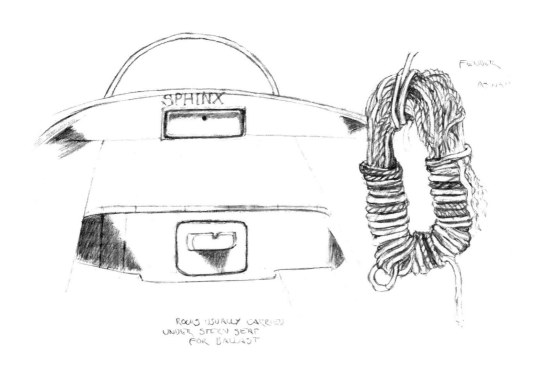

The ordinary twist is called right-handed and results in a pattern of fibers going the same way as the diagonal stroke in a "Z." In rope making, individual fibers are first twisted thus to form a yarn. Then, two or more yarns are twisted together, left-handed, to form a strand. These strands are then twisted in the final, right-handed way to form a rope.

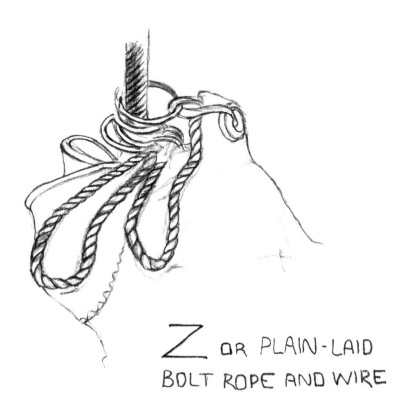

Z OR PLAIN-LAID
BOLT ROPE AND WIRE

Three-strand plain rope is unequalled for versatility in knotting and splicing. It has held its own mainly in mooring and anchoring use while the sheets and halyards of most yachts consist of a braided cover enclosing a plaited core. In the case of minimum stretch Kevlar or the rubber inside a stretchy shock cord, the core is usually straight. The braided configuration provides uniform roundness, kink resistance and pliability; splicing braided line requires special tools and a trained eye and is seldom attempted outside professional rigging lofts.

Knots may be tied equally well in both of these configurations, but the pleasure of handling them as well as the safety of the knot will be enhanced by a slightly matt rather than shiny surface finish. In quality polyester and nylon line I look for at least a partial infusion of short, woolly fibers among the endless, nominally stronger, shiny ones.

Ken Green, of Marlow Ropes at Hailsham in East Sussex, agrees that the matt Marlow ropes knot the most successfully and also untie more easily. On the subject of polypropylene, another synthetic fiber, usually seen in metallic blue or green color designed to offset its poor resistance to sunlight, he says: "Most knots will work with this material although slippage is a problem sometimes. Our most successful polypropylene has a hairy finish and seems to grip extremely well."

Hairy rope or not, the Lee High Cordage Co. of Allentown, Pennsylvania, only blesses a polypropylene knot when tied as a bowline or double sheet bend.

My advice is to stick to polyester and nylon and avoid the dead, plasticky feel of propylene and polysplit, both of which splice better than they knot.

The best practicing ground for knotting remains the working lines of the boat in use. Much is made of rope load tables but often a deck line can be selected on the basis of what is comfortable to handle. Of course, a main anchor warp needs to be substantial in any displacement boat, but if it is so big you can't handle it well it may not come up quick enough from the locker to give you a chance to use it.

In forty years of sailing I haven't had a line let go, except for a boat yard's worn-to-the-bone mast lifting strap which I was careless not to inspect before using.

As a rule, use nylon for mooring and anchor line, polyester for sheets and halyard tails and Kevlar for all-rope halyards. Kevlar, incidentally, *must* be palm-and-needle whipped most carefully to keep cover and core balanced.

To keep them supple and strong, you have to treat your lines well. Any line needs to be rested and rinsed in fresh water occasionally. At the end of the season, use a tub to rinse out damaging grit and salt crystals.

Avoid shock loads on a line—such as picking up a tow with a great jerk —and be equally wary of kinks and sharp angles. Keep what lines you can

in the locker when cruising in the tropics. Sunlight will eventually weaken all modern fiber rope.

Reverse your genoa sheets at the midpoint of each season to take persistent strain off the sheet lead section. All-rope halyards will benefit from the same treatment.

To store well-rinsed, dry rope you can make up a furling-line coil as shown in the drawing or, better still, let it fall loosely onto some battens that keep it off the floor or hull and allow air to circulate around it.

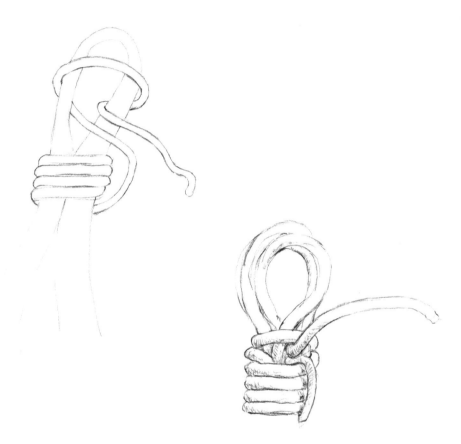

FURLING LINE COIL

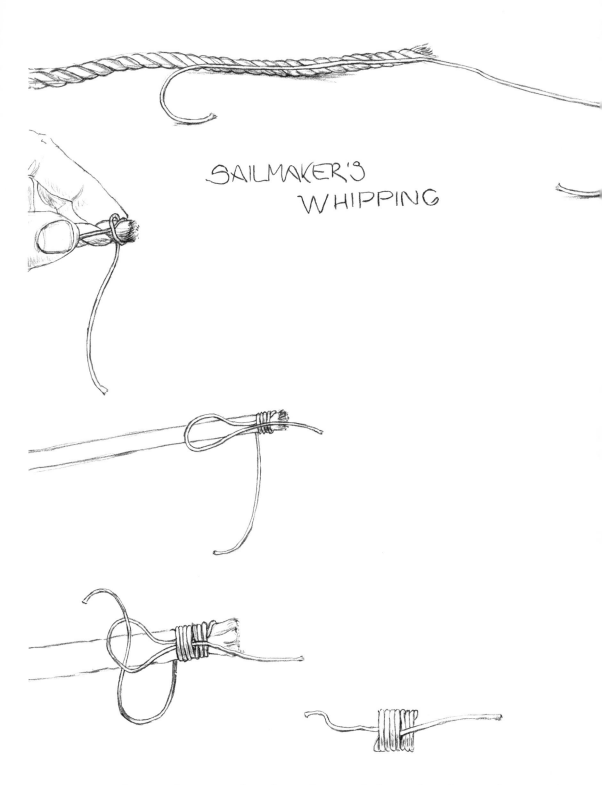

SAILMAKER'S WHIPPING

If cut, a line must be whipped around the end with waxed twine. A palm-and-needle whipping will hold for the life of the rope, but a sailmaker's whipping will do for the short term.

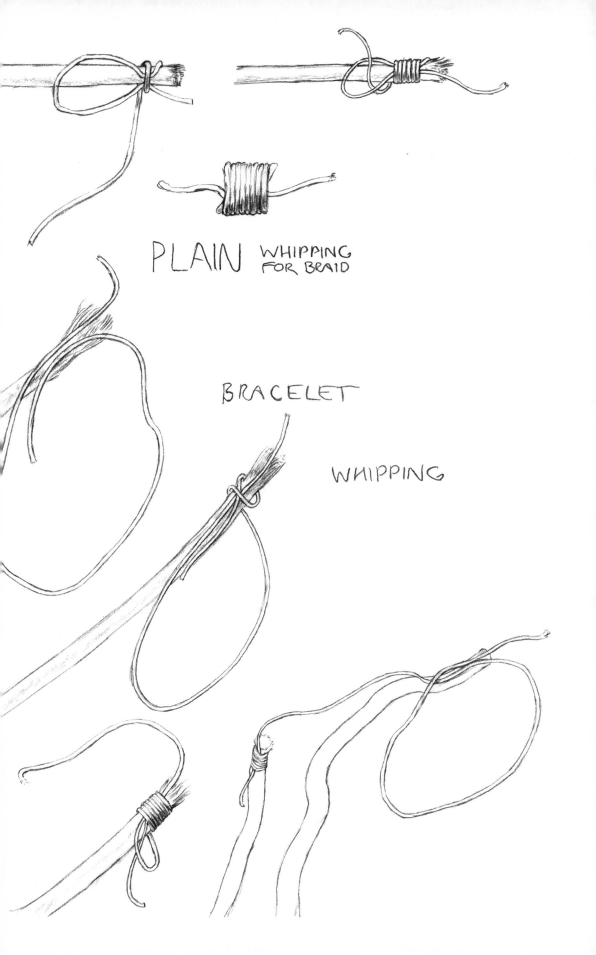

PLAIN WHIPPING FOR BRAID

BRACELET

WHIPPING

The Scottish rigger Leonard Popple has written about rope as "God's most ambrosial gift to sailors." To make it so, it must be cared for and few are the boats outside racing that can pride themselves on good, supple lines. Remember also that a reliable knot needs to be pushed, tugged, and gently persuaded into position. To make this task easy, you need good, well-cared-for rope.

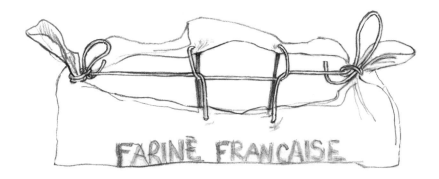

KNOT NAMES AND THEIR ORIGINS

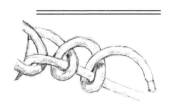

The name of a knot is often an enigma well worth unraveling. You have the square knot, which is named after a near physical parallel, as it is a square knot. You have the identical reef knot, which is so called because it's useful in tying in a reef.

In Scandinavia, neither form is current. Rather, it is consistently called a "råbandsknop."

Rå stands for a yard aloft to which a square sail is bent.

Band means a strap.

Knop is an ancient Scandinavian word from which the English word knot is derived.

So deciphered, you have a name descriptive of another long-established use, that of securing a square sail to a yard by means of a strap or line.

In German, on the other hand, you have most commonly the name "kreuzknoten" which like square knot reaches for a physical parallel, though less successfully: Kreuz means cross.

Do not infer from this that nautical language is a Babel of tongues; rather, it can be seafarers' esperanto. Witness another descriptive phrase:

English	Scandinavian	German
Round turn	Rundtörn	Rundtörn

It would be nice if all knot names were descriptive of origin and use, like in the "studdingsail halyard bend," a name which compresses all you would ever want to know about the knot into three words. Or, if at least the name conjured up a resemblance, as in the figure eight knot. Both types of naming are useful, the first making you understand the knot and the second helping you to remember it.

If a choice has to be made in referring to a knot, as with reef and square knot, I would pick the origin variety over the memory aid as it tells you (in this instance at least) a great deal about the nature of the knot. The knot is indeed better suited to finishing off a reef lashing or tie than to join two ropes (a use to which it is often put) and the name tells you as much.

Unfortunately, there are knots with names that wander off absurdly. Take the midshipman's hitch. The only midshipman I can remember is one that sat in the Telefonos office in Palma de Majorca, patiently waiting to call the mainland. He looked homesick and in no way indicated that the midshipman's hitch is a rolling hitch tied on the standing part.

Maritime nomenclature can be confusing in other ways. Take knots, bends, and hitches.

A knot, besides being a catch-all for the purposeful intertwining of line, particularly refers to a symmetrical knob such as the drawn home overhand knot.

A bend often refers to the joining of two free lines. One rope is said to be bent to another.

A hitch that secures a line to an object (such as a mooring ring), is a loop knot tied in the hand, or a knot that makes a line fast to another rope which remains passive in making the knot. However, the studdingsail halyard bend ought then to be a hitch so, while learning a useful rule of thumb, beware of exceptions.

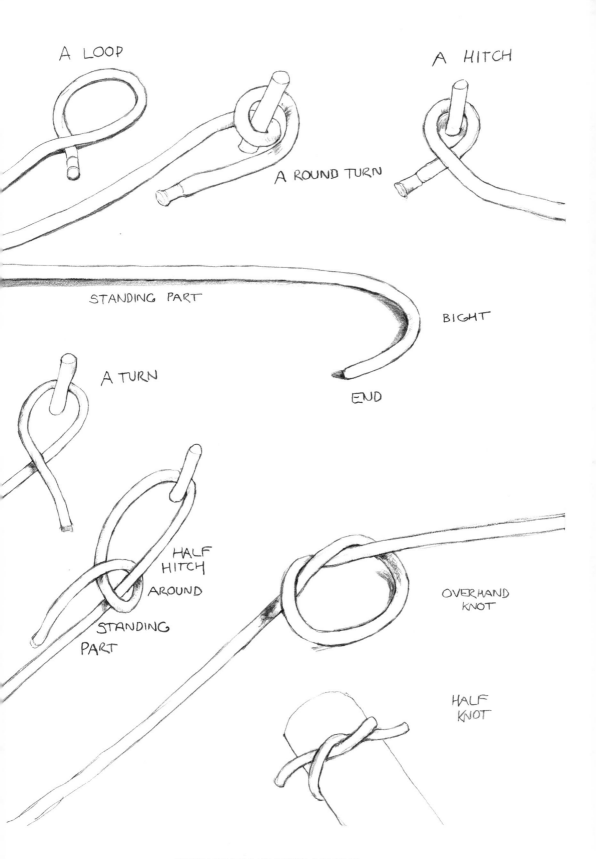

A LOOP

A HITCH

A ROUND TURN

STANDING PART

BIGHT

END

A TURN

HALF HITCH

AROUND

STANDING PART

OVERHAND KNOT

HALF KNOT

KNOT NAMES AND THEIR ORIGINS

31

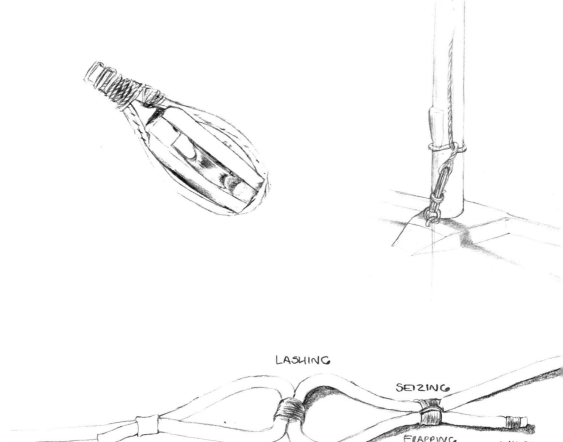

LASHING

SEIZING

FRAPPING
TURNS
ACROSS

WHIPPING

In communicating about knots it is also useful to know the exact meaning of terms like bight and standing part. Consult the drawings. As a whipping is often confused with a seizing I've added some drawings clearing up that point.

I also want to clarify the terms belay and make fast, most often used when tying a line to a cleat with figure eight turns secured with a final hitch.

Belay means to secure the rope with figure eight turns.

Make fast means to finish off with the single hitch.

The distinction is valuable if you are being hoisted to the top of the mast and in one or two unmistakable words want to tell the people down by the winch that you need a momentary pause (belay there) or want to stay where you are (make fast—which should be taken to include the process of belaying).

It is also very useful when several people without an intuitive understanding are mooring a boat.

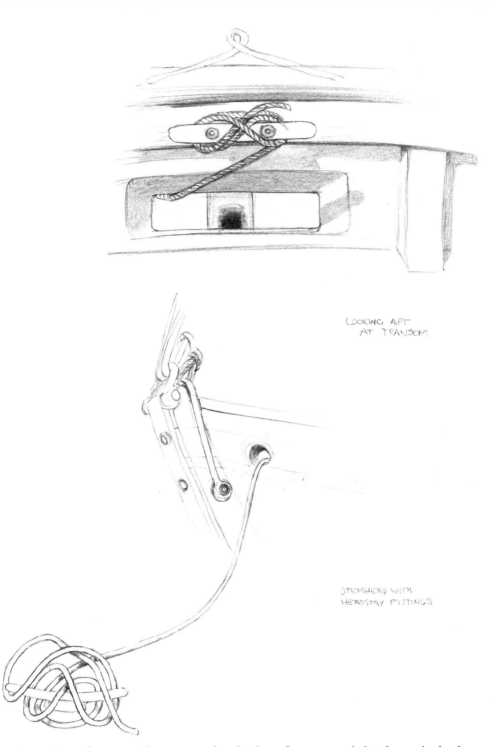

In making fast to a cleat, you take the line first around the far end which gives a clean lead and a bit of advantage if there is strain on the rope. To add to your advantage, take a turn around the cleat before commencing the slower figure eight turns. If the line fits the cleat snugly, two full figure eight turns are enough; if in doubt make it three or four. The last hitch lies more snugly if it follows the lay of the previous turns.

Sometimes, it is wise to omit the last, jamming hitch. For instance, Geoffrey Budworth tells me that a Thames river boatman belays to a cleat by means of a round turn, figure-of-eight turns, and a final round turn—"but no back hitch as the Thames has short, sharp swells and we distrusted anything that might jerk up too tight to undo in a hurry. . ."

PARTS OF A ROPING PALM

KNOTS

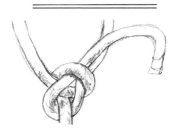

The Granny

In trying to secure a lashing or bind two ends, the first thing that comes to mind is probably a half knot followed by another half knot tied in the same direction. The resulting knot is called a granny.

In the Scandinavian languages it is known as the "kärringknop," which comes of a word for old woman, which implies that she is mean and slipshod. In Italian, it is called "nodo di vaccaio," implying that it is a knot used by people who tend cows.

My mother taught the double granny bow to me for tying my shoelaces and I expect the reader has had it instilled in him the same way. For this purpose, it is tied slipped (with the ends doubled) in the second half knot.

Although it easily comes undone, this is probably the world's most frequently tied knot. Around 1905, a professor at Uppsala University, Hjalmar Öhrwall, observed after a shopping round that of the twenty-six knots made by shop assistants in securing his packages, eighteen were granny knots. The experience made him sit down in a huff and write an excellent book about knots.

Most of us still need to make a conscious effort to avoid the granny, in favor of the more lastingly binding, symmetrical reef (or square) knot. May I recommend that the reader teach his children to use the double reef bow knot for their shoe laces?

The Reef Knot

In a reef knot, the first half knot is taken over and under, using the left-hand end. The second half knot is also taken over and under, but with the right-hand end as the lead or active part. In the granny, the left-hand end remains the lead throughout, making a lopsided knot, while the reef knot lies flat and symmetrical.

As the name suggests, it makes a snug job of tying two ends around a wad of canvas. It was as such I first knew it, rolling up the bottom of the sprit sail of the family skiff and tying together the reef lines sewn into the sail with one end slipped.

Properly drawn up and shaped, it was reliable and, given the slipped end, could be drawn off in a twinkle.

The same knot makes an excellent tie after folding a sail on the boom, both in rope and soft webbing cut in suitable lengths for sail ties.

The knot has a binding quality that benefits from the moderate strain and uniform alignment that holding a bundle entails. Using lines of different size is not permissible as there is a chance of the knot slipping to a collapse.

The reef knot is not suitable for connecting two lines as it jams up badly under strain and, worse, may collapse if subjected to a snag. The latter may be guarded against by half hitching the ends around the standing parts but then the knot becomes unwieldy.

This is a splendid knot only when used as a binding tie.

The Clove Hitch and Half Hitches

When Uncle Emil, or anyone else on the North Sea coast of my youth, tied up his boat, he did it with a clove hitch followed by two half hitches around the standing part. Like the passion for feathering the oars between strokes, it amounted to a local religion.

Of late, it has waned in that you often see the clove hitch omitted and the half hitches taken with a doubled bight—especially when a tie is made to a ring and the doubling of the lines saves you from pulling all the cordage through it.

A clove hitch is really of the same configuration as two half hitches only the first is taken around a ring or bollard while the latter are usually taken around the standing part of the rope or passed as two separate hitches—as in the drawing of a scowed anchor on the peramba *At Anapeae* at Cabo de

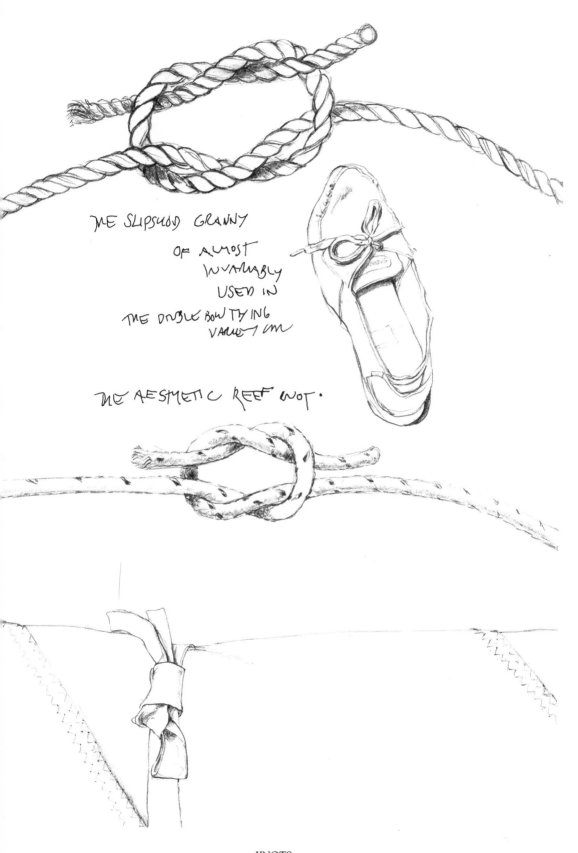

THE SLIPSHOD GRANNY

OF ALMOST
INVARIABLY
USED IN

THE DOUBLE BOW TYING
VARIATION

THE AESMETIC REEF KNOT.

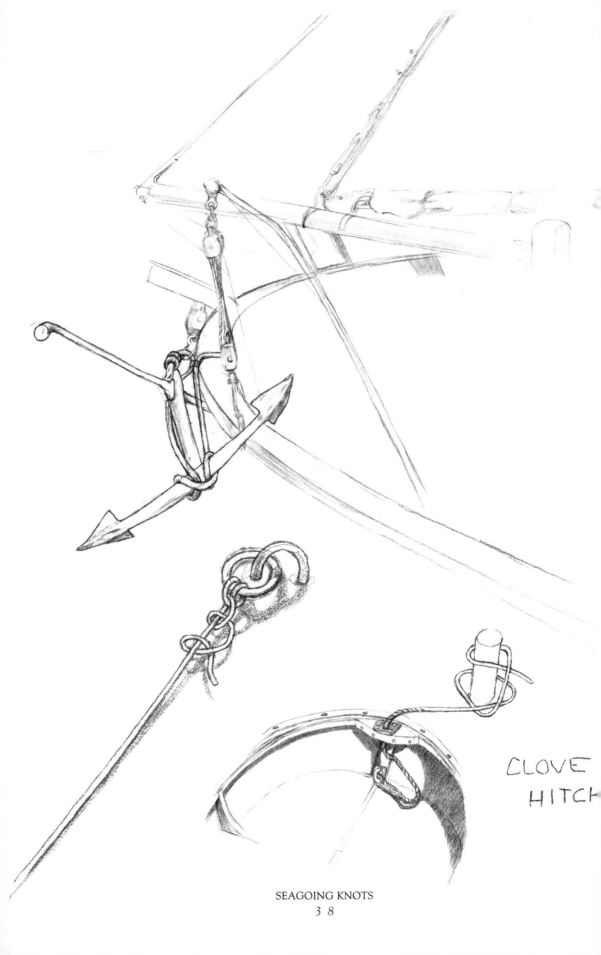

CLOVE
HITCH

Crio in the eastern Mediterranean. Omitting the rudder stock, it converts to a clove hitch.

You may say that a clove hitch is a jamming form of two half hitches. It follows that if a clove hitch is taken around a bollard of great girth, it will not jam effectively and becomes unreliable, unless secured with half hitches on the standing part. But even around a ring, I would add the half hitches for peace of mind.

A use well suited to the clove hitch by itself is shown in the view of the permaba's mainmast and shrouds. To rattle down, that is, lashing the rat-lines to the shrouds to make a convenient ladder aloft—the clove hitch is ideal, holding tight over the small girth of the individual shroud.

A strong case could be made for reviving "ratline hitch," a traditional name for the clove hitch that has sunk into oblivion. It is both colorful and descriptive of proper use.

Seeing that the clove hitch has to be supported when used as anything but a temporary docking tie, we turn again to half hitches on the standing part. Used by themselves, they too are best around a ring or similar slim object. They tie well in this way but there is a threat of them jamming hard if any great strain is placed on the line. Moreover, when tied to a flogging jib clew, the half hitches tend to come undone.

Rather than prefacing them with a clove hitch, you can start with a round turn or backhanded hitch around the object or through the ring. Of these, the backhanded hitch in particular secures against jamming, and both give the line some initial haft which greatly improves the chances of the succeeding half hitches to survive high wind and water.

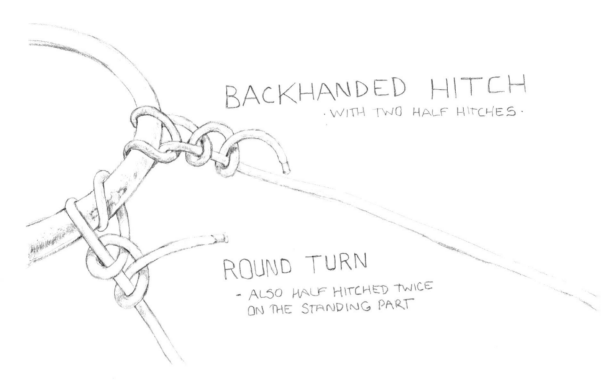

BACKHANDED HITCH
·WITH TWO HALF HITCHES·

ROUND TURN
- ALSO HALF HITCHED TWICE
ON THE STANDING PART

The round turn has the added advantage of taking up strain on the line as soon as it is passed through and can also be used to slack off under full control when there is a strong pull on the rope.

Yet, faced with a bollard that dwarfs my mooring line, I would still revert to the religion of Uncle Emil.

The Bowline

The bowline owes its name and possibly its conception to the need to securely fasten a line to a bowline cringle and thus trim the leech of a square sail. This knot, unattended in lofty rigging, had to be proof against collapse and, in spite of constant strain, unlikely to jam.

The basic version is a fixed loop, but tied to the standing part it will also make a suitable sliding loop; or, when two unequal lines meet, two interlocking bowline loops can be relied on.

Another way to join lines—preferably equal ones— is to overlap the ends of lines and tie bowlines onto the standing part of the opposite line.

My grandfather taught the bowline to me and his other grandchildren with an air of genuine respect. The older ones were the first to be initiated and we who were youngest looked forward to our turn with impatience if not awe. The old man did not bother with the "rabbit goes into the hole and around the tree" version of tying it but went straight to the quicker and more elegant "flip-over" style of tying, as will I.

Find a supple length of rope for tying. To live up to its very high potential, the bowline needs to be worked into a balanced, snug shape and a stiff line will not allow that to happen.

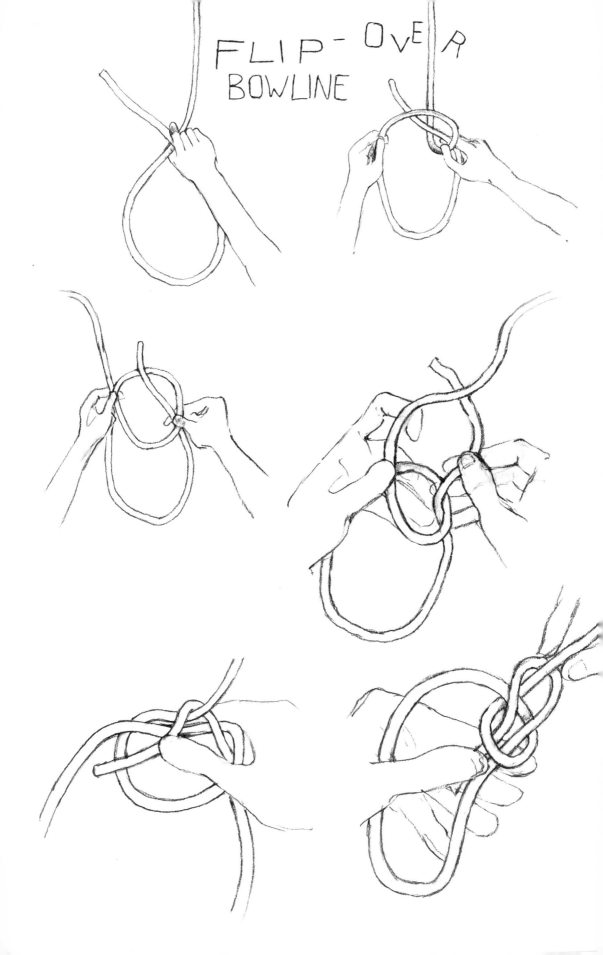

FLIP-OVER
BOWLINE

The Flip-over Bowline

The drawings are arranged from left to right, from top to bottom.

Face the line and make a loop with the end on top of the standing part. With the juncture grasped between thumb and forefinger and your other fingers bearing on the standing part (second drawing), twist your right hand away from you so a loop is formed in the standing part.

Into this, the end naturally falls (third drawing).

Flip the end behind the standing part and down into the small loop (fourth and fifth drawings).

To finish, push the line snug around the standing part while pulling at the end (last drawing).

Manipulate until tension in the knot is well balanced.

As the name I make bold to use for it (there being none firmly established) implies, the flipover must not be tied in ponderous stages but in one flowing sequence. Slap down the end on the standing part with enough impact to start the twisting process, let the end remain alive as it flips up into the small loop formed and see that it continues without a pause around the standing part and back down into the loop.

The only moment of contemplation should come at the end when you work the knot into shape.

To loosen the bowline, push the standing part back into the knot. This takes the strain off all parts of the knot simultaneously.

The Bowline Stopper

In a quiet anchorage on the Baltic Sea, I once shared some delicious pan-fried herring with a Stockholm gentleman in a very narrow and very elegant skerry cruiser. Having treated me to the herring, with tart lingonberries on the side, he popped over another tidbit, a stopper turn for the bowline end.

The bowline, as is previously said, is safe on its own if tied to suitable line and snugged up properly. But there are times, when the safety of the boat or a crew member depend on it, that you want to add something.

Rather than a simple half hitch, use this stopper, which consists of an overhand knot on the end taken around the bight as shown in the drawing. It lies very snug against the bowline without straining it.

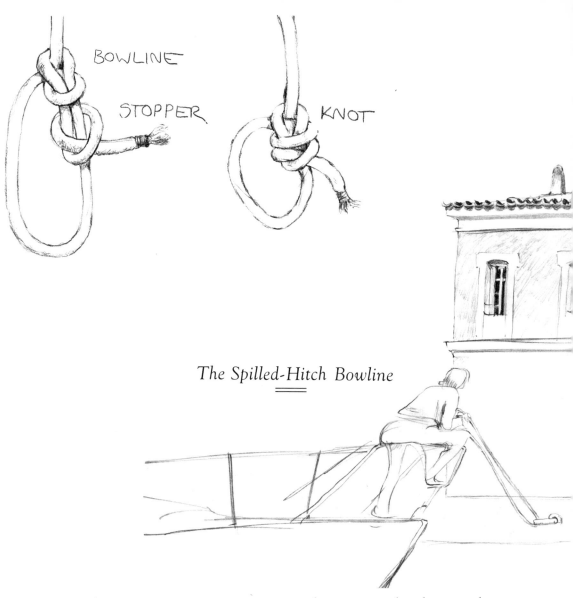

BOWLINE

STOPPER

KNOT

The Spilled-Hitch Bowline

There are times, coming into port, when you just barely get a chance to pass a line through a ring and need to tie your bowline facing the shore rather than the standing part of the line. You must then go from the flip-over to the spilled-hitch bowline.

Pass the end through or around the object to which you want to make fast. Then, as shown in the first drawing, take a hitch around the standing part. Ease the standing part away from you with your left hand while putting a counterclockwise twist in the end with your right (second drawing). With such persuasion, the hitch will spill over on the end as in the third drawing.

The end is then passed behind the standing part (fourth drawing) and snugged up as in the final view.

This version of the knot never attains the speed and elegance of the flip-over but has a simple virtue in a tight spot, and can even be used when there is a bit of strain on the standing part.

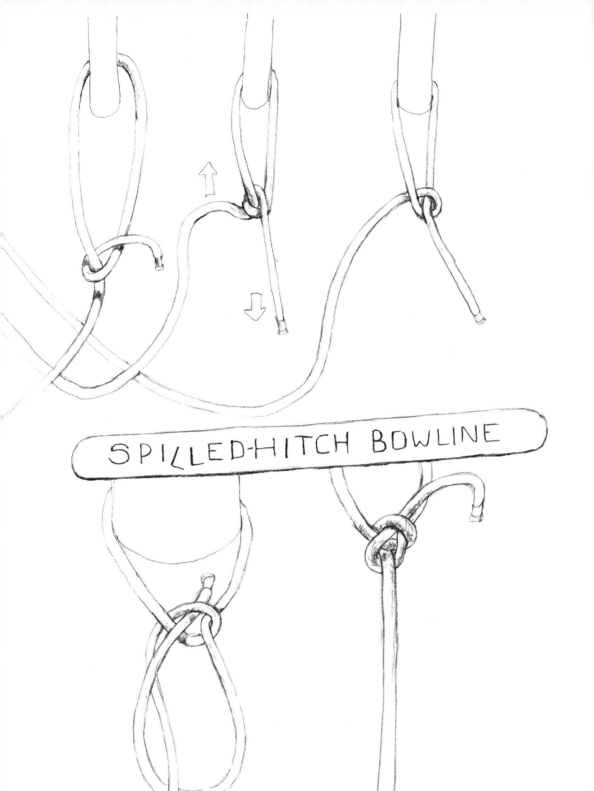

SPILLED-HITCH BOWLINE

The Bowline on the Bight

An on-the-bight bowline may be tied with a doubled end anywhere along the line.

If tied near the end, the two-loop configuration can be used as a primitive bosun's chair, with the short bight under a man's arms and the long one under his hind quarters.

Using a doubled end, start off as with a flip-over bowline but do not take the end around the standing part.

Instead, at the juncture shown in the first drawing, fold the end loop back, enveloping the knot. Then work the loop up snug around the standing part, adjusting the resulting two loops to desired size.

If a man is to be suspended in it, the end may be attached to the standing part with a bowline or rolling hitch.

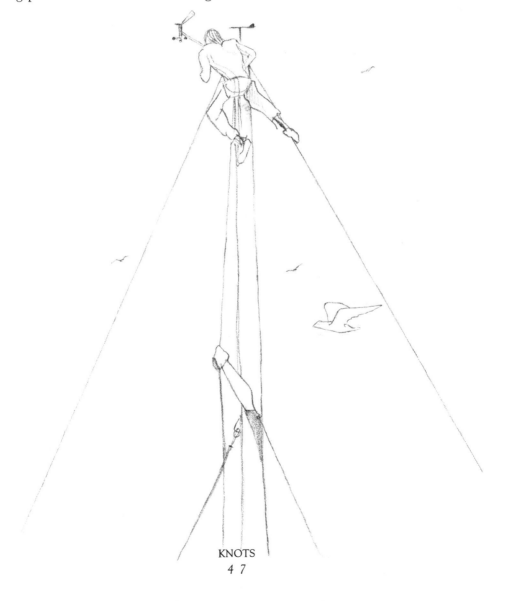

Another use for this simple and ingenious knot is to attach the middle of a spring line to a bollard ashore when one end is already cleated at the bow or stern and you want to save the trouble of reeving all the line through to make, say, half hitches. In this instance, the two loops are adjusted to equal size.

The Sheet Bend

I held out for years against the sheet bend because it looks too simple to be reliable. But one day in the Ionian, the Falmouth Quay punt *Twilight* ghosted into the town quay of Gaios on Antipaxos and took the remaining, awkward berth between *Moth* and Spiro's excursion boat.

To keep the boat in position, a spring line was needed and Spiro, breaking off his nap under the cotton sun awning over the *Blue Grotto Taxi*, passed it to a pink complexioned, spruce old man by the tattered blue ensign on the punt. This individual took the proffered line and quickly made a bridle by attaching two lines of his own to it. The punt, rakish bowsprit and all, lay snug.

The newcomer, dressed in dark blue sweater and loosely flapping khaki shorts, saluted his neighbors with a wave that suggested the awkward grace of a British officer.

Colonel Bertram Bloomer, Royal Engineers, ret., had demonstrated the simple fact that a sheet bend will accept three lines. A squall during the night, without so much as a nudge from *Twilight*, demonstrated that the knot could be relied on.

The sheet bend derives its name in several languages (Scandinavian: "skot-stek;" German and Dutch: "schoten-stek" and "schooten-stek") from its traditional use in holding the sheet to a becket in the clew of the headsail.

As this is the most flogged knot on the boat, other testimony to the tenacity of the bend is hardly needed. Suffice to say that the basic configuration is the same as that of the splendid bowline and that a sheet bend can even be tied by the same method.

A single sheet bend ties best in roughly equal size and otherwise compatible rope. Like the bowline, it does not tie well in stiff rope.

Whenever a sheet bend is tied, make sure the ends come out on the same side of the knot. Otherwise, the geometry is wrong and the knot unsafe.

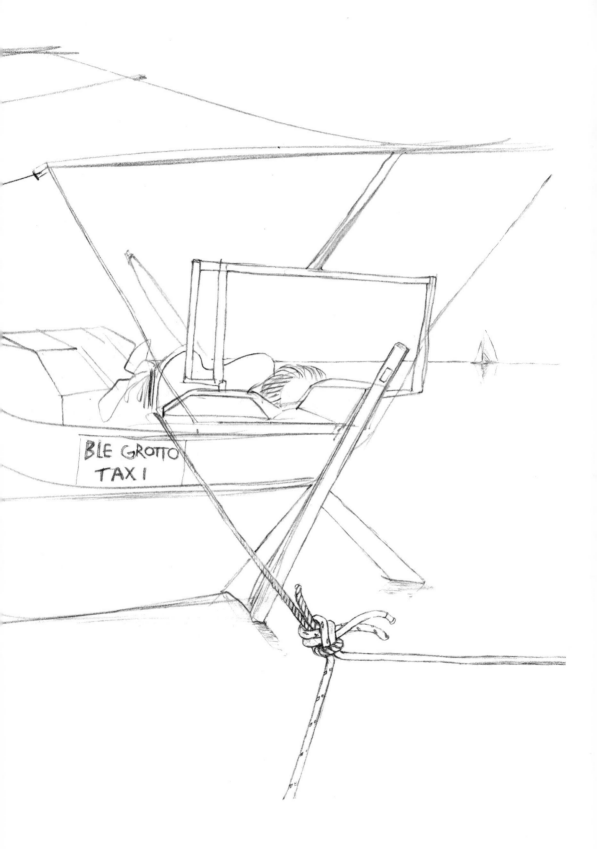

BLE GROTTO
TAXI

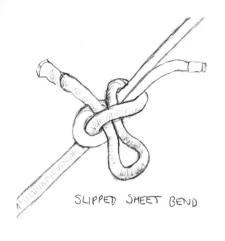

SLIPPED SHEET BEND

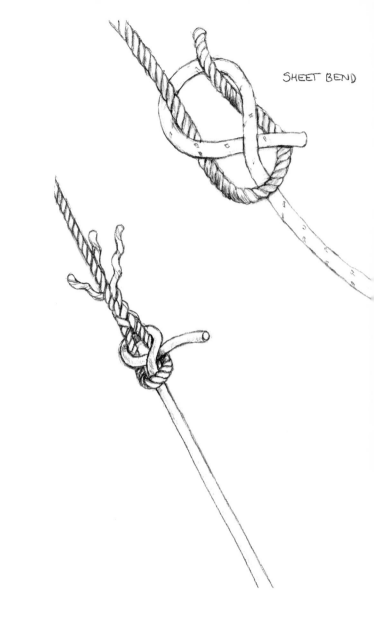

SHEET BEND

STARTING POINT:
BOWLINE

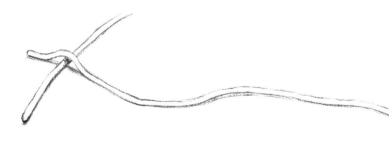

STARTING POINT:
SHEET BEND

SEAGOING KNOTS

NAXOS APPROACH

The Flip-over Sheet Bend

Note the difference in "starting position" between the flip-over bowline and ditto sheet bend. I would advise the reader to become proficient in the flip-over bowline first. The execution of the knots is the same, with the difference that the bowline makes a fixed loop and the sheet bend joins two lines.

Take one line end in each hand and place as in the drawing showing hands position. Twist your right hand clockwise away from you, making a

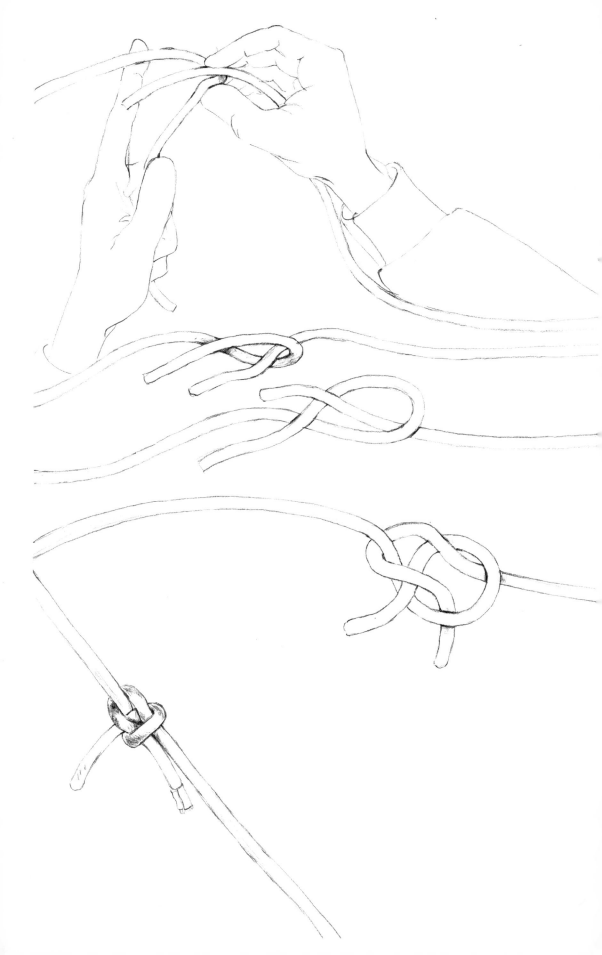

loop in the left hand line as the end of the right-hand one is popped up into it (second and third drawings).

Keeping up its momentum, flip the end around the back of the left-hand line and into the center loop (fourth drawing).

Be sure to snug up the knot well as this is essential for the holding power of the knot. With the flip-over mode of tying, the final knot will look a little funny but if you turn it around it will present the usual sheet bend look, only mirrored.

Single, Double, and Tucked Sheet Bends

The single sheet bend can naturally also be tied by doubling the heavier line and tucking the lesser one into it. This mode of tying becomes the only practical way if you want to take an extra turn to make a double sheet bend.

The first double version shown is more secure than a single sheet bend, especially when the lower line is finer and lends itself to additional turns. Also, it is less likely to jam.

The second double sheet bend shown is called for in quick work as the end is tucked only once. It unties quickly, too.

The tucked sheet bend is identical to a single one, only the end of the white line in the drawing is looped and tucked in the same direction as the

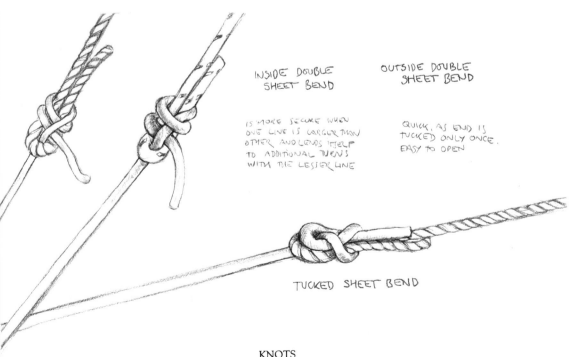

INSIDE DOUBLE
SHEET BEND

OUTSIDE DOUBLE
SHEET BEND

IS MORE SECURE WHEN
ONE LINE IS LARGER THAN
OTHER AND LENDS ITSELF
TO ADDITIONAL TURNS
WITH THE LESSER LINE

QUICK, AS END IS
TUCKED ONLY ONCE.
EASY TO OPEN

TUCKED SHEET BEND

other end. The tuck streamlines the knot and makes it less subject to snag, especially if the ends are lashed or taped over.

The Double Sheet Bend Variation

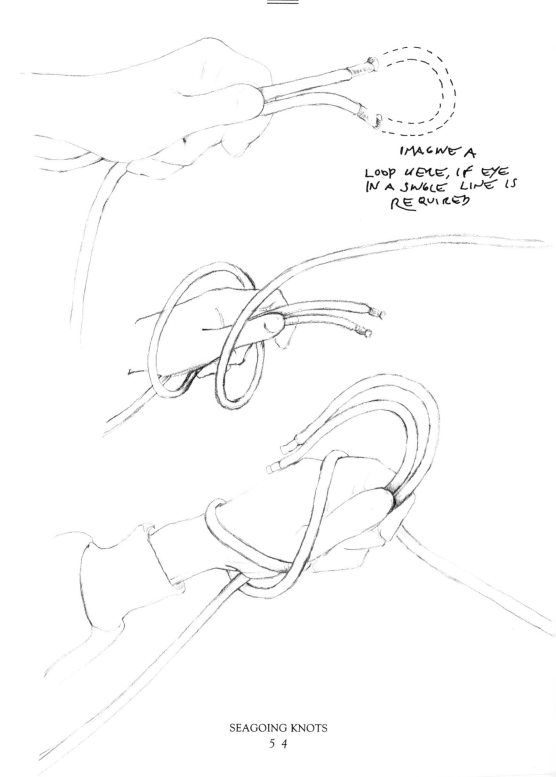

IMAGINE A LOOP HERE, IF EYE IN A SINGLE LINE IS REQUIRED

Bertie Bloomer (of Senglea, Malta) also knew a different double sheet bend, with a mode of tying that lends itself to light throwing lines and the like. It joins two ends but will also make a reliable fixed eye in the bight of a single line. The directions are the same for both varieties, except that in the first instance you hold up the ends of two lines to be joined (first drawing) and in the second you have a single line, with a bight of it held up as a loop (dotted line in first drawing). The directions that follow will bear on the first instance.

Wind one of the lines—the lesser one if there is a disparity—to make two turns around your hand as shown in the second drawing. Flip the ends of the lines back as in the third sketch, let go the doubled line and draw your hand back far enough to grab the ends anew (fourth drawing). Maintain the general position of the lines as this is done and firm up the knot carefully (last drawings).

One advantage of this double sheet bend, as well as of the bowline and sheet bend flip-overs is that you very soon tie them by rote, quickly and well, however dark the night or evil the sea.

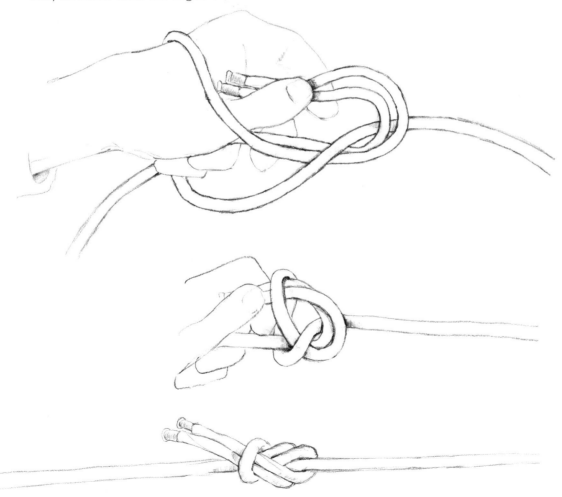

The Heaving Line Bend

If there is a great disparity in size between lines that need to be joined, the single and double sheet bends become unbalanced and therefore unsafe.

The answer is the heaving line bend, which will join a light messenger line to rope. As shown, figure eight or "racking" turns pull the thick end snugly together before the knot is finished off with a half hitch on the standing part of the thicker line.

HEAVING LINE BEND
— OR RACKING BEND

MAY BE LOOSEN UNDER LOAD

The Rolling Hitch

Moth was anchored with line and chain in a small blind alley in the north end of Nisiros which is euphemistically called the harbor.

Dusk was coming on when the still air was rent by a whistling puff of wind out of the north. We paid no great heed, but when a number of men came sculling out to their fishing boats, their punts frothing at the bow, we had to.

I told the crew we might have to spend the night at sea, whereupon an Indian gentleman urgently asked to be put ashore. He just needed to pack his dressing gown, toiletries, and slippers. By the time he was heading for the local hotel all but one of the fishing boats had steamed off, heading for the shelter on the other side of the island, and an ugly six-foot sea was running straight into the anchorage.

Abandoned ground tackle was floating everywhere amidst the froth and each black sea made *Moth* rear like a nervous stallion.

There being no anchor winch, the anchor line was laid textbook fashion on the main forward cleat. Nonetheless, the line was jammed beyond

human powers. The kitchen knife purchased at Izmir came out and we cut loose and cleared out, blessing the locals with another CQR.

Some time later, entering Heraklion harbor on Crete before a foaming nor'easter, a trabaccoli man took our line and tied it at an angle to a convenient hawser, introducing me to the rolling hitch.

If I had had the pleasure before Nisiros, the anchor would still be with me.

The rolling hitch happily ties at an angle to another line and, unless very slippery cordage is involved, holds tenaciously. Thus, a line jamming on a cleat or a sheet with overrides on a winch drum can quickly be relieved of strain and put to rights.

A cruising man from Tolleshunt D'Arcy in England, Michael Vinnicombe, told me it was his favorite knot when we bumped into each other one stormy night in Dover harbor.

"I use it to attach my anchor light to the forestay and have found no other knot that will do it," he said. Mr. Vinnicombe's high opinion is no doubt justified, especially as the knot ties simply and well.

When a rolling hitch is secured to another rope as in the drawing of how the Nisiros situation could have been handled, the second turn taken with the end is jammed inside the first. This creates an override which prevents the knot from sliding sideways.

If tied without this jamming override, the knot can be used as a tie but may well slide.

The rolling hitch is sometimes called a clove hitch with an extra turn. The Italians even have this idea incorporated in the naming of the knots, calling the clove hitch a "nodo parlato" and the rolling hitch a "doppio parlato." "Nodo" means knot and "doppio" double. Where the "parlato," or talking, comes in I cannot say.

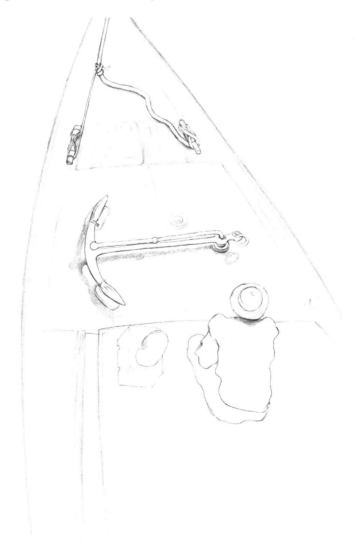

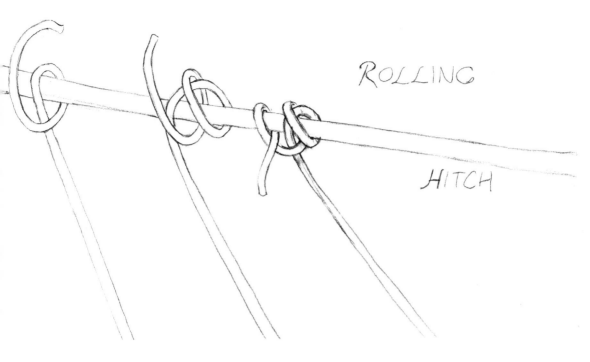

ROLLING

HITCH

The Midshipman's Hitch

This knot is a rolling hitch tied on the standing part to make a fixed eye. Cyrus Lawrence Day, in *The Art of Knotting and Splicing*, advises a man who has fallen overboard and is being dragged through the water at the end of a line to use it as it can be tied with the line under tension.

Be that as it may—in most man-overboard situations a safety harness would make a better starting point than a rope eye—in mooring situations the midshipman's hitch often makes a more straightforward tie than the bowline if there is a strain on the line. It will start to hold actively as soon as the second turn has been jammed in. For a temporary fix of the eye, it is enough to hold the end snug against the standing part.

To be left alone in safety, the end needs to be half hitched around the standing part just like the rolling hitch usually is.

The drawing shows the knot from the point of view of Day's desperate case, but if it is turned upside-down you will see it from the more commonly recommended point of view of a man tying up to a bollard ashore and who uses it to get some strain off the end.

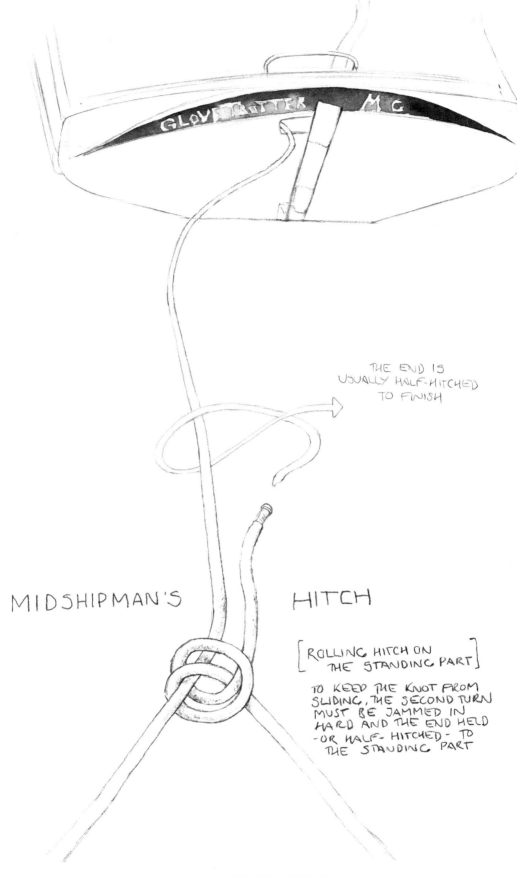

THE END IS
USUALLY HALF-HITCHED
TO FINISH

MIDSHIPMAN'S HITCH

[ROLLING HITCH ON
THE STANDING PART]

TO KEEP THE KNOT FROM
SLIDING, THE SECOND TURN
MUST BE JAMMED IN
HARD AND THE END HELD
-OR HALF-HITCHED - TO
THE STANDING PART

Lark's Heads and Toggles

Sometimes, the extensive use of a single type of knot on a boat proves instructive. I had never taken any interest in the grapevine knot until scrambling on board the ischetano trawler *NA 179*. Every knot on board was a grapevine. The skipper had even dodged the need to use another tie for his mooring lines by splicing and toggling them.

Nor did the lark's head make any waves until I stepped on board my good friend Olaf Gilka Damm's 8 Meter *Margaret* to sail from Skagen to Marstrand. Olaf had found the boat laid up in a shed at Robertson's yard on the Clyde. He bought her from the elderly owner, Mr. Dumfries Ballentine, who provided Olaf and me with a favorite maritime character in his notes about the history of the boat since the 1927 launching.

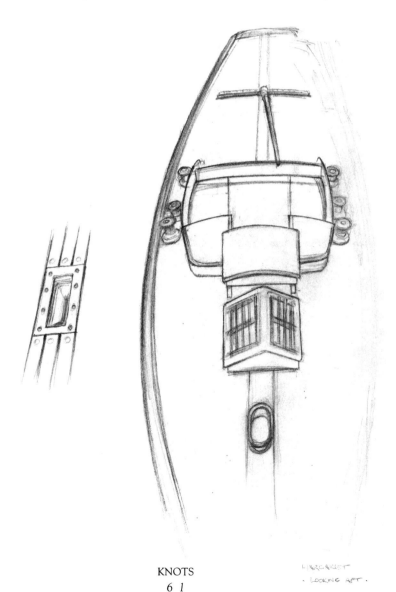

MARGARET
- LOOKING AFT.

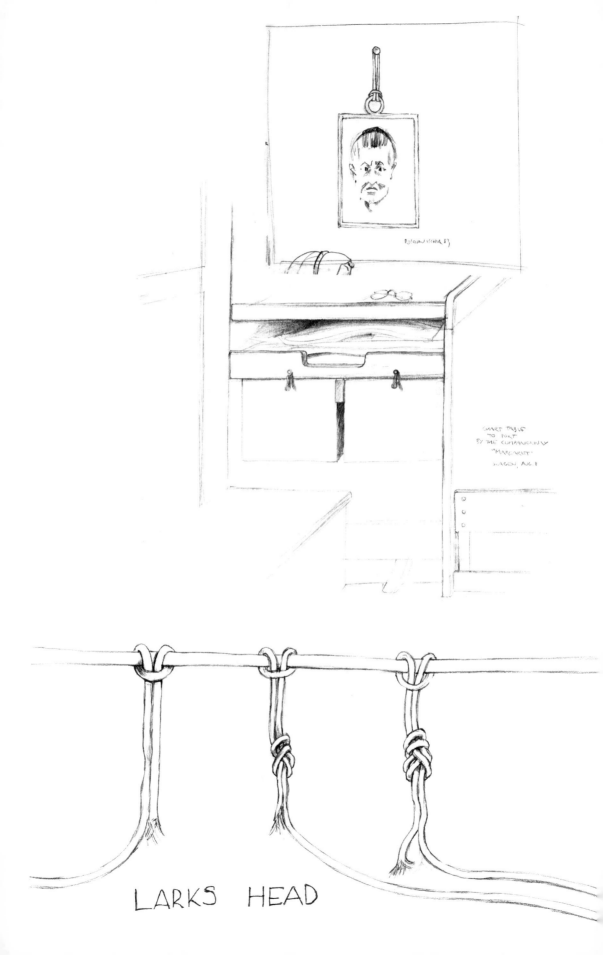

CHART TABLE
TO PORT
BY THE COMPANIONWAY
"MARGUERITE"
BEACON, AUG. 8

LARKS HEAD

MARGARET

"My brother and I raced and cruised her right up to the outbreak of the war in 1939. At that time we had a paid hand who was known as 'Tar-brush.' He came from the east coast of Scotland and was most disrespectful but a most excellent seaman. He got very drunk on occasion."

The knot favored by Olaf was the lark's head. It served for everything from hanging pictures and implements to slinging the mainsail ties to the lifelines.

To join lines reliably, he often had two eyes meeting in a lark's head.

Where a safe but quick release coupling was needed, he would permanently attach a sling to the object, as instanced by a lead weight in the drawing, and putting the sling into a loop at the end of the main line, pop the object through.

Later, I adapted the system to attach a varying number of lead weights to the snatch block that rides down *Moth's* anchor line to give a better angle of pull along the bottom.

In a couple of places, Olaf also used the lark's head as a conventional tie for the end of a cord, letting an overhand or figure eight knot transfer the pull on to the single part—as seen in the drawing.

On board *Margaret* I also noticed the skipper's duffel bag which had a flip-over top which neatly closed with a couple of toggles.

REAL "DUFFEL" BAG

As it happens, lark's heads and toggles make an interesting and useful combination.

In the drawing, lines have been joined with, from top to bottom:

Toggled bight
Toggle and eye
Bight and eye

Either way, you have a connection that can be cast off in a moment by withdrawing the toggle. There must, of course, be a harmony between the size of the lines, bights, and toggles. The more snugly they can be worked, the more reliable the arrangement.

The toggle must be carved from sound hardwood such as oak or hickory and may be fattened in the middle to allow a groove without impeding its strength.

The traditional sailing ships used toggles aloft and on deck but these days even the duffel coat seems to be on the skids. The more the pity, as many a fixed-length lashing, on deck at least, could be well secured with a toggle or toggle-and-lark's-head arrangement. Even "Tarbrush" would approve, I warrant.

The name of the knot has no relevance unless you take Professor Öhr-wall's point of view and consider that the completed knot, viewed from the side, is reminiscent of a bird's head.

To give your imagination even freer rein, consider the Italian name of the knot: "boca di lupo," which suggests the mouth of a wolf!

LARK'S HEAD WITH TOGGLE   TOGGLED BIGHT
TOGGLE & EYE
BIGHT & EYE

EYE TO EYE MAY BE MADE
IN THE SAME WAY AS
LAST TWO, IN THE MIDDLE
SUBSTITUTING AN UN-
ATTACHED TOGGLE

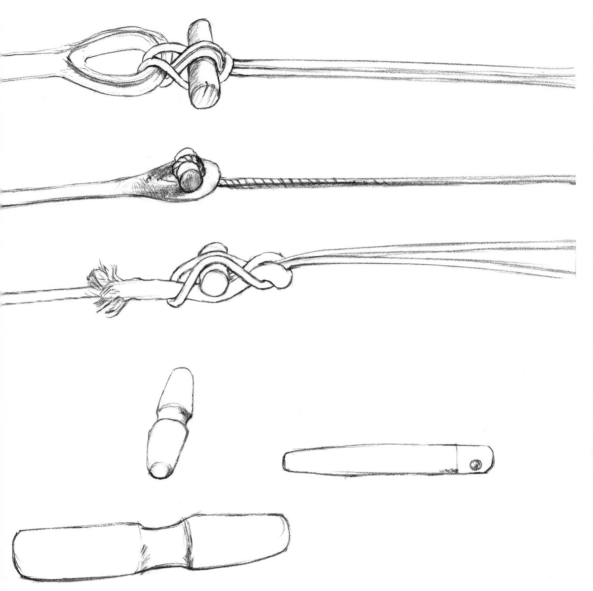

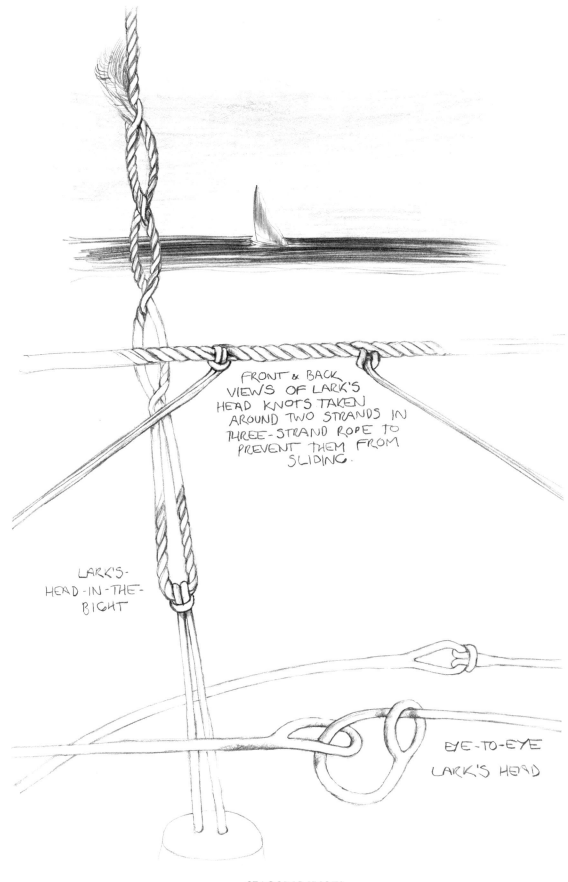

FRONT & BACK VIEWS OF LARK'S HEAD KNOTS TAKEN AROUND TWO STRANDS IN THREE-STRAND ROPE TO PREVENT THEM FROM SLIDING.

LARK'S-HEAD-IN-THE-BIGHT

EYE-TO-EYE LARK'S HEAD

The Marlinespike Hitch

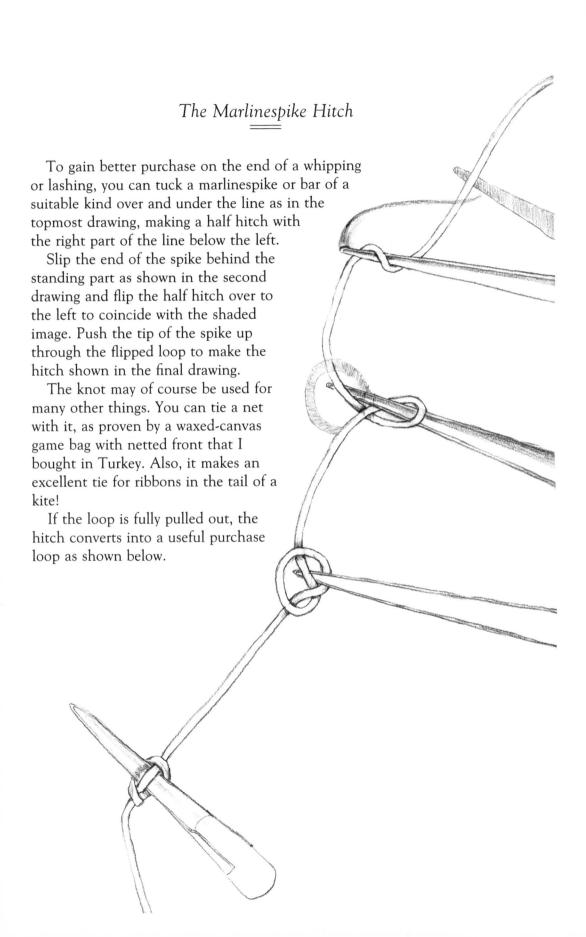

To gain better purchase on the end of a whipping or lashing, you can tuck a marlinespike or bar of a suitable kind over and under the line as in the topmost drawing, making a half hitch with the right part of the line below the left.

Slip the end of the spike behind the standing part as shown in the second drawing and flip the half hitch over to the left to coincide with the shaded image. Push the tip of the spike up through the flipped loop to make the hitch shown in the final drawing.

The knot may of course be used for many other things. You can tie a net with it, as proven by a waxed-canvas game bag with netted front that I bought in Turkey. Also, it makes an excellent tie for ribbons in the tail of a kite!

If the loop is fully pulled out, the hitch converts into a useful purchase loop as shown below.

The Purchase Loop

You are cordially invited to a Formula 40 launching at Dana Point. Gino Morelli, the designer, is there, and you may glimpse the shining pate of Alex Kotzloff, the physicist who kept the Little America's Cup cat trophy in the U.S. for so long. We will focus, however, on Rick Blethem, a young man in Navajo Indian sandals who used to build Kevlar nose cones for NASA space rockets.

As soon as the boat hits the water, Rick starts to set up the rigging. The mast is raised with ordinary cordage and set to the rake and position it will have under sail.

To firm up the lines so the wire rig may be cut to the right length on the spot, Rick employs a purchase loop knot. Thereby, he gains a double purchase.

The strain on the tail of the rope is so slight that he hazards fastening it with several half hitches further down the line, as seen in the drawing.

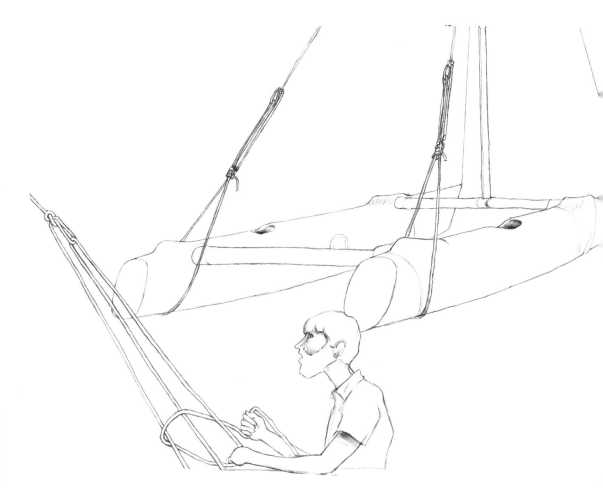

To tie the knot, you make a loop as seen in the first detail drawing, then stick another bight through and snug up as in drawings two and three. Finally, to gain the purchase, take the end around a suitable anchorage and back up through the loop most recently made.

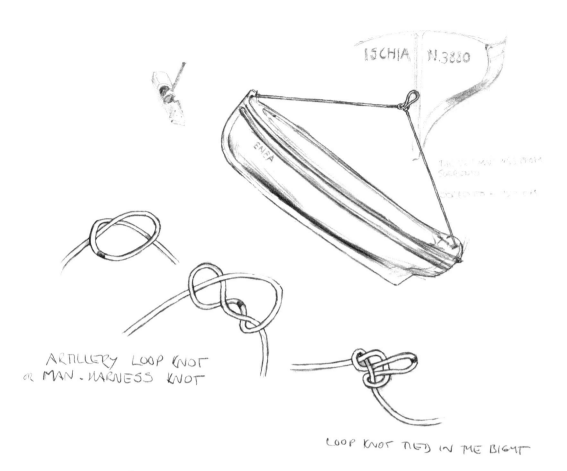

ISCHIA N.3880

ARTILLERY LOOP KNOT
or MAN-HARNESS KNOT

LOOP KNOT TIED IN THE BIGHT

I use the arrangement on my Scandinavian Duckling one-design to haul tight the luff of the jib, and it works very well.

As the loop can be made anywhere along a line without access to the end, it may prove handy in hoisting or lashing down a dinghy or simply gaining a hand hold on a line. It is sometimes called the artillery loop knot, the name being derived from such use in field of battle maneuvers.

The Figure Eight

The basic figure eight knot, once known as the Flemish knot, is best used as a stopper at the end of a line. Put to such work, it is a little bulkier than an overhand knot and will not jam quite as hard under tension. This handsomely symmetrical knot is tied as shown by the left hand line in the top drawing.

Much less known is the bend variety of the same configuration. To tie it, you start with a loosely made figure eight knot, then take another line (right hand line in the top drawing) and enter it where the working end of the other line exits. Follow the configuration of the left hand line until you get to the standing part, as shown in the second drawing from the top.

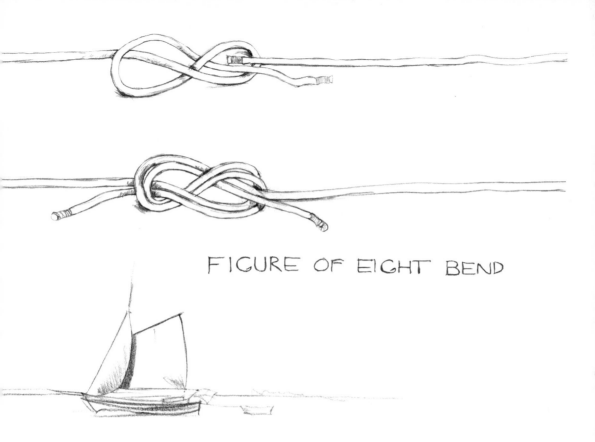

FIGURE OF EIGHT BEND

This bend will join two cords or light lines pretty snugly and the bend does not usually jam beyond redemption. In larger line, the knot becomes rather bulky and unwieldy but remains a useful bend. In particular, it has a virtue in that once you know the figure eight stopper, you cannot fail to tie the figure eight bend correctly.

The same applies to yet another variety, the figure eight eye. This is tied just like the figure eight knot, except that you use a doubled end. It does not jam as easily as an overhand eye and holds well unless the end and the standing part are forced apart. An overhand knot joining them gives added security.

Of late, the knot and its varieties are called simply "figure eight." I opt, privately at least, for the more traditional and deservedly stylish "figure of eight" name, while stopping short of the less informative "Flemish knot" variety.

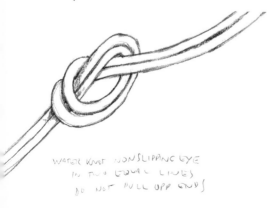

WATER KNOT NONSLIPPING EYE
IN TWO EQUAL LINES
DO NOT PULL OPP ENDS

FIG 8 WILL NOT
SEIZE UP.
MAY BE USED IN
OUT WITH LARKS HEAD.

The True Lover's Knot

Tropical storm Josephine had been upgraded to a hurricane. It was reported 200 miles northeast of Nassau, with 75-mph winds and 16-foot waves. Playing it safe, we tucked in behind Nassau's Potter's Cay, next to James McKinsey's *Jatea* of Ragged Island and Moodey Moxey's *Glove Trotter* of Moxeytown, Andros. Moodey, a jaunty old man with a skipper's cap hoisted well aloft on his sparse white curls, had brought in 2,000 conch shells at one dollar a conch and was the only sober man on board.

"I run de boat back and go from Porgee Rocks to Gibson Cay when we get dem five hundred chicken on board tonight," he yelled against the high whine of the wind.

A sturdy paddle came floating along on the agitated water and Moodey made a bight in the end of a line, took turns around the standing part and the end, and tucked through (see drawing), whereupon he bent down over the ultramarine topside and slipped the noose over the handle. Snugged up, and with a half hitch to lock the noose, the knot comfortably held the flotsam as he hoisted it over the side.

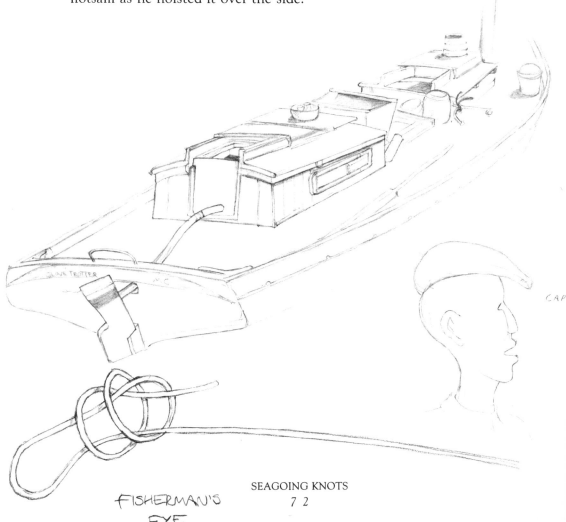

FISHERMAN'S
EYE

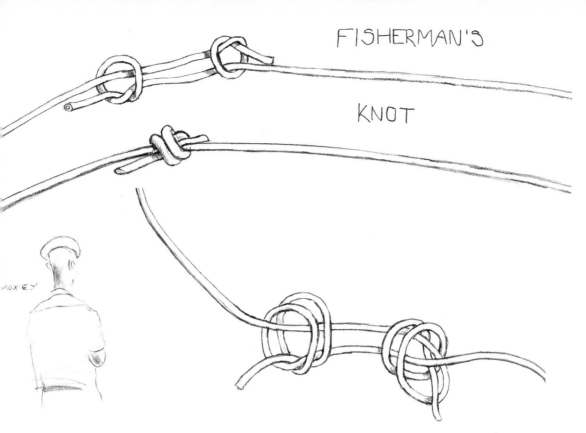

MOXEY

"But what can I co do with dese fellows, mon?" he said, pointing the paddle at his cousin Welton, who grinned sheepishly under a newly purchased knitted cap with bands of bright yellow, violet and green.

"Dat no child's play, mon!"

The knot was a double overhand on the standing part, best known as a fisherman's eye, which if loosely tied, will make a running noose that snugs up comfortably around a floating object by simply pulling at the end.

The basic configuration used is that found in the more common fisherman's knot—which is called a knot but is by definition a bend when it joins two ropes. The rope ends are overlapped and overhand knots made on the opposing standing parts. It ties well in all rope dimensions, and holds well but jams pretty hard. The lines joined should be reasonably compatible. . .and, you guessed it, it is also known as the true lover's knot.

The configuration lends itself to joining slippery, synthetic cordage lines. In my youth, it was tied in lengths of plastic-covered wire to hold drying fish on drying stands on the island. I never saw a fish fall down.

To increase security, for, say, trailing warps, or tying Kevlar lines together, make it a double fisherman's knot, which is then called a grapevine knot.

Again, this knot ought to be called a bend, for uniformity's sake, but let us rather honor the exceptions, especially as there is another knot called the fisherman's bend. In any case, it was one half of the grapevine knot that Moodey employed in his rescue mission.

The Constrictor Knot

On stepping over to *Glove Trotter's* orange deck before its perilous chicken delivery (which was successfully effected), I noted a fine demonstration of the constrictor knot in the cord that lashed the neck of the deck pump. The canvas scoop was held bravely by the knot shown. It can be applied whenever a tenacious grip is needed.

Mr. Michael Vinnicombe claims it can be used instead of "jubilee clips" (hose clamps) in emergencies.

To get sufficient purchase, you will probably need to wind the ends of the cords around pegs of wood.

When contemplating this kind of knot, remember that soft and stretchy lines tie better around a hard object like a mast or stanchion than does a stiff rope.

PAR, GOVERNMENT HOUSE GROUNDS, NASSAU O.T 2?

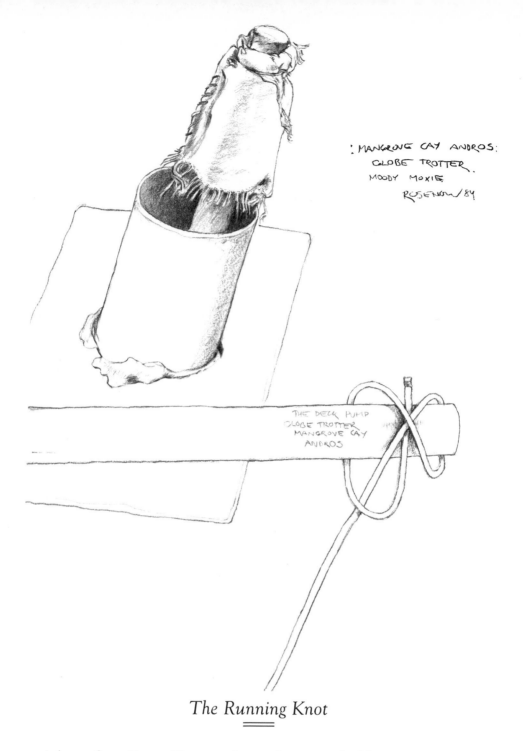

MANGROVE CAY ANDROS:
GLOBE TROTTER.
MOODY MOXIE
ROSENOW/84

THE DECK PUMP
GLOBE TROTTER
MANGROVE CAY
ANDROS

The Running Knot

A letter from Bertie Bloomer dropped in recently. He wrote:

"The return trip from the Ionian was rather marred by an unfortunate accident in the middle of the night 100 miles from the nearest land and 180 miles from Malta.

"We were hit on the stem by a freighter in spite of all that my one crew and myself could do to avoid her. I am quite certain that he was on automatic steering, which was hunting a bit, and that nobody was on lookout. I feel also, but have no proof, that he was some sort of gun runner. However, he did stop and stand by us for a couple of hours whilst we sorted ourselves out.

"The whole of the top part of the stem was completely smashed, which, of course, meant that there was no forward support to the mast. Fortunately, because of the enormous strength of her construction, *Twilight* was not making a very serious amount of water, and I managed to pass a running knot under the forefoot and bend it, secured, to the jib halyard.

"Later, this also allowed us to set the staysail. I then decided we should be able to at least make Sicily under sail if not Malta. Without the jib she would not go to windward very well if in a lumpy sea, but at least with the staysail we could heave-to in the event of bad weather. With considerable help from my fairly new little 13-HP diesel, which gives me a far greater range than the old petrol engine, we in fact made Malta. As I said to one of the locals looking at her lying on her mooring, she looks like the title of a book on wartime Malta, *Battered But Not Beaten*."

Simple and effortlessly tied in a dark Mediterranean night, this running knot may prove helpful sometime. Tie it as shown and you have about the simplest adjustable eye you can make. In the basic form (first two drawings), it can be used to tie up a horse or, as I saw in the village church at Laki on Crete, to hitch the bellringer's rope to the bottom end of the church's lightning conductor.

But, if finished with a stopper knot similar to the bowline stopper previously mentioned, either above or below (as shown in the third drawing), the basic knot is made secure and that is the way Bertie did it.

I feel bound to record that, since the above was written, there has been a tragic postscript to *Twilight's* plucky story. In Bertie's own words:

"During the last two or three years I have found that with my increasing age the upkeep of *Twilight* to my standards was beginning to prove too much for me, and I just could not keep her and see her deteriorating.

"As a result I had arranged to give her to a deserving, part charitable school in England for adventure training. The school is, in fact, closely connected with the Royal Engineers in which my army life was spent.

"I set off from here with a good crew to sail her back to the UK. In spite of rather poor weather we had a good trip via western Sicily, southern Sardinia, the Balearics, and were 790 miles on our way.

"We grounded on the south coast of Spain in what according to the most up-to-date charts was 15 fathoms of water just outside a large, attractive bay with good shelter. The cause of the trouble was vast quantities of mining waste pumped out to sea.

"It proved impossible to move *Twilight* and soon after a bad storm completely destroyed the boat and resulted in her total loss."

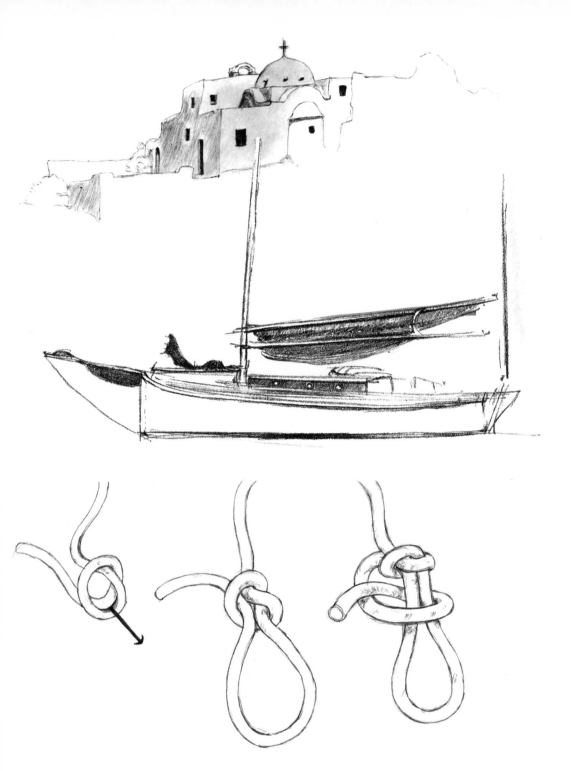

Fortunately, Bertie and his crew were taken off in time and suffered no physical harm.

The nighttime grounding of *Twilight* occurred at Puerte de Portman, east of Cartagena, and she was the third yacht lost in similar circumstances.

The Anchor Bend

Harry Summers, formerly a *Popular Mechanics* subscriber of Norfolk, Virginia, had anchored *Nerissa* somewhat perilously on the exposed side of Leros Bay. Yet his fair-haired little daughter (the original Nerissa) played unconcernedly on deck and the boat presented a picture of tranquil domesticity. A nautical eye might have faulted the lack of gaff and boom on the Turkish-built craft, but not the snug arrangements. Harry explained the missing gear:

"We discarded the boom after a few years to get rid of weight and clear the deck and then, since the gaff and heavy cotton sails still proved unwieldy, the gaff went too, whereupon there was no need for sails.

"We were aiming to go down the African coast but be it for lack of sail or whatever, we came only as far as Port Said."

Having discarded much of the gear aloft, Harry did pay attention to his ground tackle, using heavy cable securing his anchor line with a knot that I recognized from Uncle Emil's time.

It was called the "flaggbānd" (the flag bend) and was in favor on the island for bending on the national flag. It had the reputation of a very reliable knot.

It is shown tied around the anchor flukes merely to show the configuration rather than for any nautical motivation.

"Snug it up good, and it won't fail," said Harry, going back to his *P.M.* collection below.

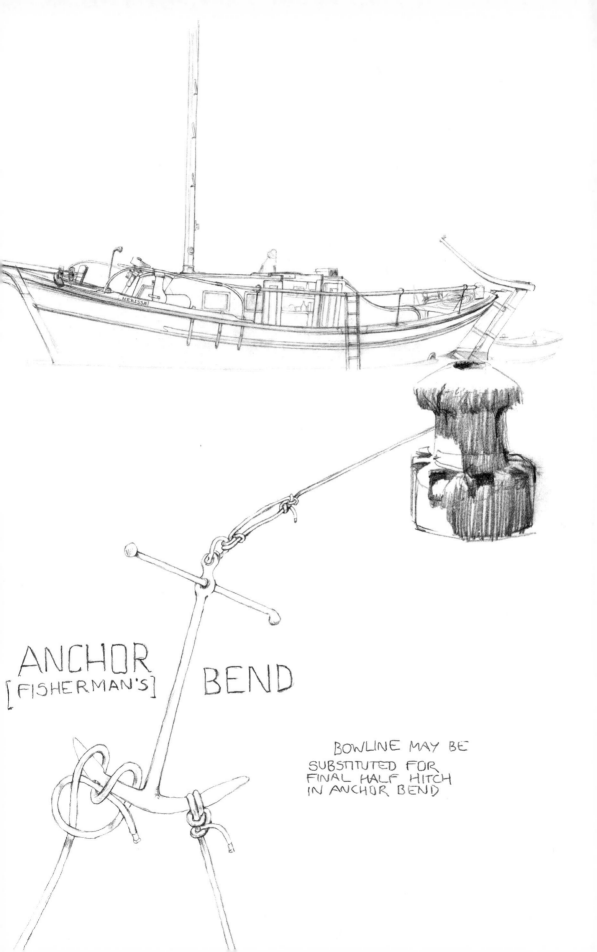

ANCHOR
[FISHERMAN'S] BEND

BOWLINE MAY BE
SUBSTITUTED FOR
FINAL HALF HITCH
IN ANCHOR BEND

The Studdingsail Halyard Bend

Having so far displayed only practical, sober knots, I beg indulgence with the studdingsail halyard bend.

It may be but a relic of a richer maritime scene, the glorious name says it all, but it is close enough relation to the anchor bend to need differentiation, and may yet come in handy when belaying securely to a horizontal bar.

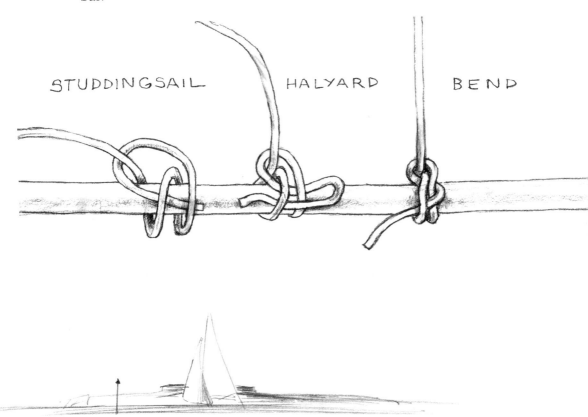

The Timber and Killick Hitches

It was mid-November, and a wintry gale was blowing when Bill Farley and I left Southwest Harbor on Mount Desert Island, Maine, Fort Lauderdale bound. The boat was the 49-foot Hinckley *Morning Star*, owned by Otto Morningstar of Boston, Massachusetts.

She carried a pre-production version of the Hood Yacht Systems roller-furling gear (this was back in the mid-1970s), power sheet winches and the odd convenience like ice maker and color television. The ice maker we did not need, but we were glad to have brought long johns and navy surplus "destroyer pants" as the temperature dropped and the wind increased during the first night out.

The gale was out of the north and as I steered the boat downwind and down wave just after midnight, it was exhilarating to have the squad boat race on the crest of great waves, a rooster-tail of Atlantic froth off our quarter. We were under full main and full genoa, but with the wind increasing every minute and a buttery feel to the wheel, it was time to reduce sail in order to make a broach or jibe less catastrophic.

Bill, of Raleigh, North Carolina, the best shipmate anyone could wish for, appeared in the hatchway at the moment I had decided to call him out.

"She wants a bit of harnessing, I think," he said.

We began to reduce on the roller genoa first, given the single furling line, which could quickly be laid on a power winch.

What exactly went wrong, I don't know. Suffice it to say that the winch hesitated slightly at one point and rather than investigate we gave the power button another tentative stab. This resulted in the spectacle of seeing the whole roller furling gear—which incorporated the forestay—part with the mast top and crash into the sea ahead of us.

By rights, the mast should have followed, but thanks to the pressure of the wind on the mainsail and because the spinnaker halyard had been taken to the bow pulpit, it stayed up. With the furler sausage and a mess of lines under the boat, the boat lurched to a near halt. Waves from astern were breaking over the counter and there was a good chance of fouling the rudder and the propeller.

Bill quickly put another couple of spare halyards on the bow before I dared bring the boat into the wind. With one wave after another crashing over the stern, Bill managed to get a hitch around the heavy genoa sausage as it floated up alongside. The next time it surfaced, he made a death-defying dive over the leeward lifelines to get another hitch around the heavy bundle, dogging the end around the standing part a couple of times.

The end of the line went on the power winch. This time, it did the job and helped us get an otherwise unmanageable load onto the rail. "It is a tie we used when hauling logs down in Oriental [North Carolina]," said Bill as we chugged toward Boston under diesel power. "I've always wanted to test it again." The knot was in fact a killick hitch, the most reliable form of the timber hitch.

May I add that Hood, egged on by Otto Morningstar, quickly came round and put the furler to rights, and that our midnight ride is the only Hood Systems failure I've ever heard about.

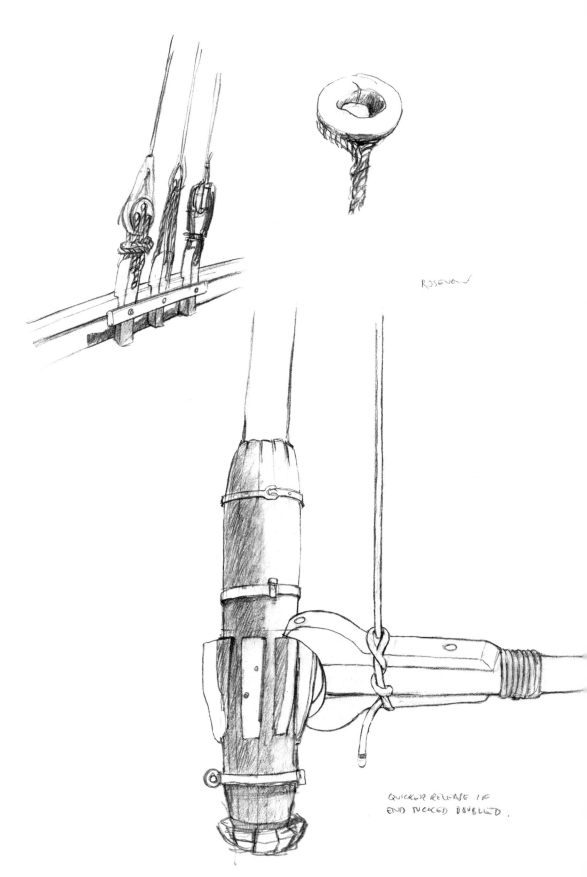

ROSEVOU

QUICKER RELEASE IF
END TUCKED DOUBLED.

SEAGOING KNOTS

8 2

The Studdingsail Tack Bend

There is only one road on Long Island in the Bahamas. The Queen's Highway is long, narrow and hot. By the time you pass the Scots Presbyterian Church on a dry bluff to your left, you probably wish you had stayed in Clarencetown with your boat rather than wander about, an easy prey for the sandflies. I wipe the sweat from my brow.

A few days earlier, Howland Bottomley, at Regatta Point on nearby Eleuthera, had complained about knot tying standards in the islands. "Among young Bahamians with their fast outboards and other go-fasts there seems to be a complete ignorance of knots. The granny is so well liked that you see it tied from one end of a line to the other!

"The half hitch is commonly used to bend a line on an anchor or to tie up to a piling—but sometimes there are as many as four or more hitches!

"The more infrequently visited locales show a lack of knot tying ability."

Farther along the bone-dry road, where it passes through the infrequently visited locale of Deadman's Cay, I find Rupert Knowles hacking out weeds with his machete, occasionally glancing across the shimmering, white road at the ten-foot-wide stern of a newly built Bahamian sailboat hull, propped up beside the shallow bay by a kitchen table and a rusty oil drum.

The topsides are painted white with bands of bright green, blue, and red. Like ribbons on a girl, that is how Rupert thinks of the stripes. To make 'em beautiful. She is not the first boat he has built since he started at age twenty-five, but it is on the edge of his mind that he will be seventy, two weeks next Tuesday, and that she may well be his last. Gout and arthritis, them no child's play, mon.

As I appear at Paul the Greek's corner down the road, he rises and walks over to the boat where there is shade under two leafy cork trees. Close up, I see that his very light blue eyes are set in bright red sockets and that he has not shaved for a day or two.

In 1961, he built a boat and went across the sound to Regatta Point and competed in the Out Island regatta, a racing series started by American sailors for local workboats. He was beaten, beaten because already the winners were not workboats but built for the race.

He had laughed then. "I'll come back next year and beat the shit out of them!" And that is what he did, with a new boat, and sails cut on his own floor.

He called the boat the *Tida Wave*. As any Bahamian schoolboy knows, it is to this day seen as the "fastest boat in the islands."

As we talk under the cork trees about sail seaming, beeswax and knots, we happen on the subject of a lasting tie between the sheets and headsail clew. Rupert takes a piece of string out of his pocket and ties a studdingsail tack bend.

"It stay put," he says.

And so it does. Even under incessant flogging, as the second hitch is locked in more positively the harder the knot is pushed against a clew or an eye. I have since used it on headsails and have had it hold when two half hitches would have flogged themselves off in minutes.

The knot is also known as the buntline hitch from its use in fastening the end of the buntlines, which on square riggers were used to hoist a square sail before furling.

In Scandinavia, the knot is known as the "flagg-bänd" (flag bend), denoting another use where its unique qualities can shine. The knot consists of two reversed half hitches on the standing part. If both turns are taken lightly, it makes a running noose. If the second turn is nipped hard, making a bulge on the standing part as shown in the drawing, you have a marginally secure fixed eye which instantly can be converted into a running noose by pushing the half hitches together on the standing part.

Lastly, the Marlow Rope people say the knot holds well even in Kevlar.

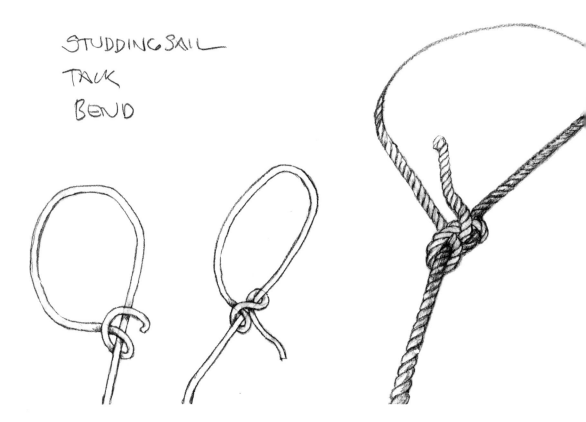

STUDDING SAIL
TACK
BEND

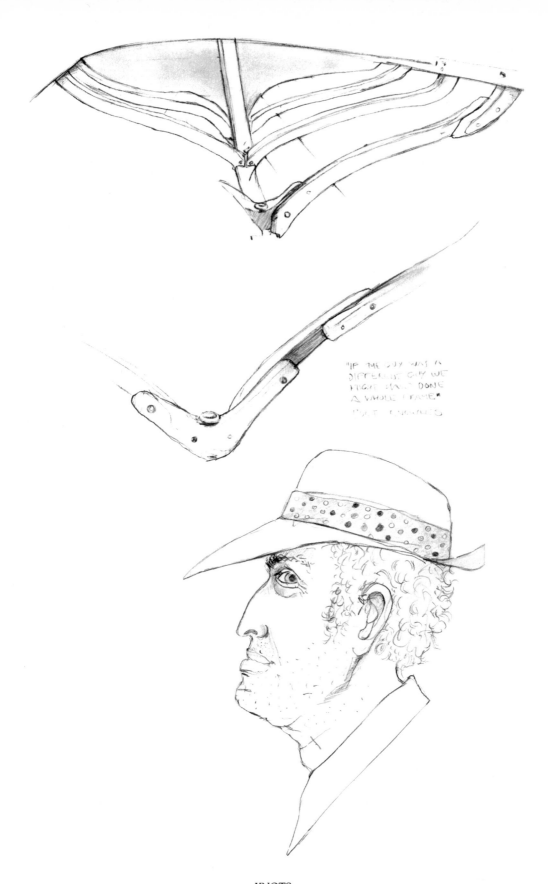

"IF THE GUY WAS A
DIFFERENT GUY WE
MIGHT HAVE DONE
A WHOLE FRAME"

The Marling Hitch

One summer afternoon in Kas, the yacht *Whisper* sailed in under a skinny-looking, battenless mainsail, en route from the Galapagos Islands, French Polynesia, Vanuatu, Bali, Christmas Island, and South Yemen.

A 14-foot Chilean sculling oar was lashed to the deck but when the wind gave out just inside the breakwater, Margaret Roth got into the dinghy and towed the 35-foot boat up to the quay. "Hal likes us to come in under our own power," she said, deadpan.

In the days that followed, my white sloop and the black-hulled *Whisper* sailed over to the blue grotto on Kastellorizon Island and up the pine-clad, mountainous coast of southern Turkey to Fethiye Bay. There, we found a natural spring under ancient Lycian tombs and, rafting up for the night, dragged all across the bay on *Whisper's* small Danforth.

All the while, Margaret, the daughter of a British engineer in the Bombay Port Trust, impressed the crew of *Moth* not only by her finishing school grace but also by her impeccable seamanship.

It was when we tucked in the sails for the night, the boats rail for rail, and saw Margaret help lace up the main on *Whisper's* boom, that I realized the difference between the chain and the marling hitch.

The marling hitch is used for lashing up ("marl down") sails, hammocks, and awnings. The point, as seen in the drawing, is that you pass the end down and through with each hitch (rather than up and through as with a series of half hitches which makes a chain hitch).

Each marling hitch in effect makes an overhand knot which holds better than a half hitch, jamming the outgoing part of the rope against the canvas after each hitch is hauled taut.

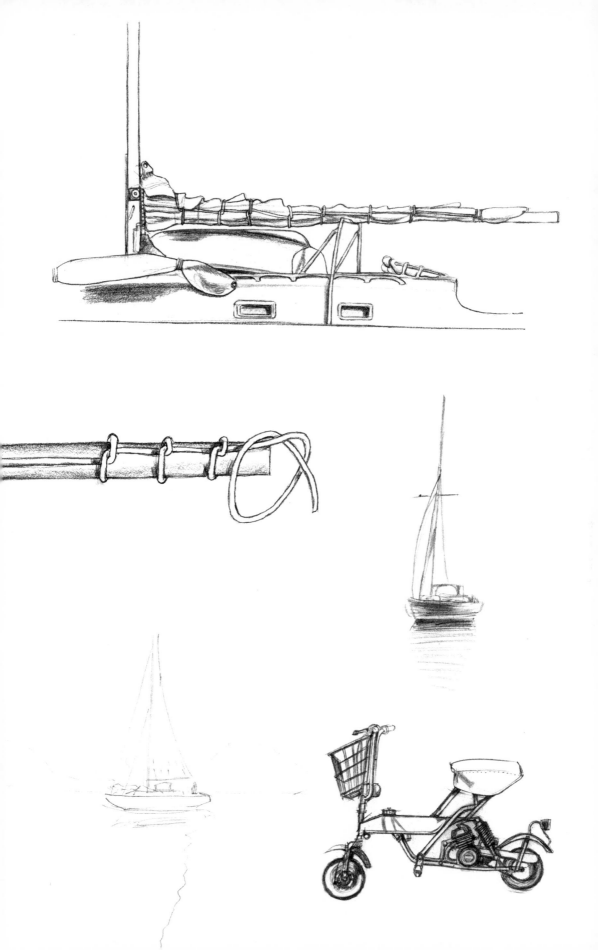

Slipped Knots

One man is down early on the low riverbank of the Nile. With the pale blue sky still tinged with crimson, Akasha Falifa Mohammed Mahmud begins to lay out his new sail on a level, sheltered piece of ground at the water's edge. With a pair of tailor's shears, he cuts each cotton panel to length as he lays it down, squinting hard with his one good eye at the result.

"Salaam." Akasha's boat boy, Ahmed, slides down from the high river bank, scattering kingfishers from among the bushes.

It is meet for every felucca man to have a boy. With a boy stationed amidships, in charge of the centerboard, the yard tackle, and the boom hoist, the main man need never leave the tiller and the mainsheet, a fortunate circumstance, as we shall see.

Having finished the sail, as the sun travels over the Valley of the Tombs of the Kings, Akasha fetches a tin of red lead paint from the cuddy forward and betters the outline of the watchful eyes of the mythological falcon Horas which gazes from the bow of his boat. In flowing script, in spite of a bristling brush, he then traces up the Arabian characters for Onass. His hand hesitates when he is to fill in the name again where it is written in Roman letters. Here, this writer is able to render some assistance and, with a courteous gesture, is invited to partake of the new sail tryout.

The river wind from the north blusters a bit but there is nothing to prepare you for the brutal weather helm that the shallow, barn-door rudder induces. Even less am I able to cope with the wrenching pull from the three-part mainsheet. No fancy cam cleats here, not even a cleat on deck.

Ahmed smiles complacently from the windward rail as Akasha unobtrusively takes over the helm. He does not even try holding the tiller but controls it by bracing his bare feet against the muski-wood leeward rail and keeping the tiller against the small of his back. The mainsheet is tamed in a twinkle by jamming the doubled end in a slipknot, as the drawing shows.

Taking our cue from Akasha's slipped half hitch, there is in fact a slipped version of all the other essential knots: the square knot, the clove hitch, the sheet bend and the bowline.

They are a serviceable lot whenever quick release is of the essence and the only wonder is that they are not used more frequently. Once you begin to employ them, there is no turning back.

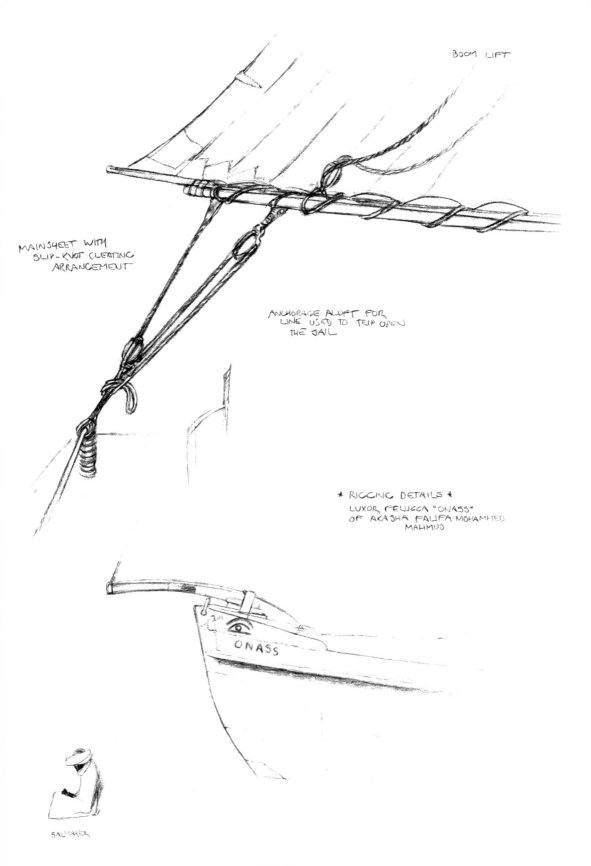

BOOM LIFT

MAINSHEET WITH
SLIP-KNOT CLEATING
ARRANGEMENT

ANCHORAGE ALOFT FOR
LINE USED TO TRIP OPEN
THE SAIL

* RIGGING DETAILS *
LUXOR FELUCCA "ONASS"
OF AKASHA FALIFA MOHAMMED
MAHMUD

ONASS

SAILMAKER

KNOTS
8 9

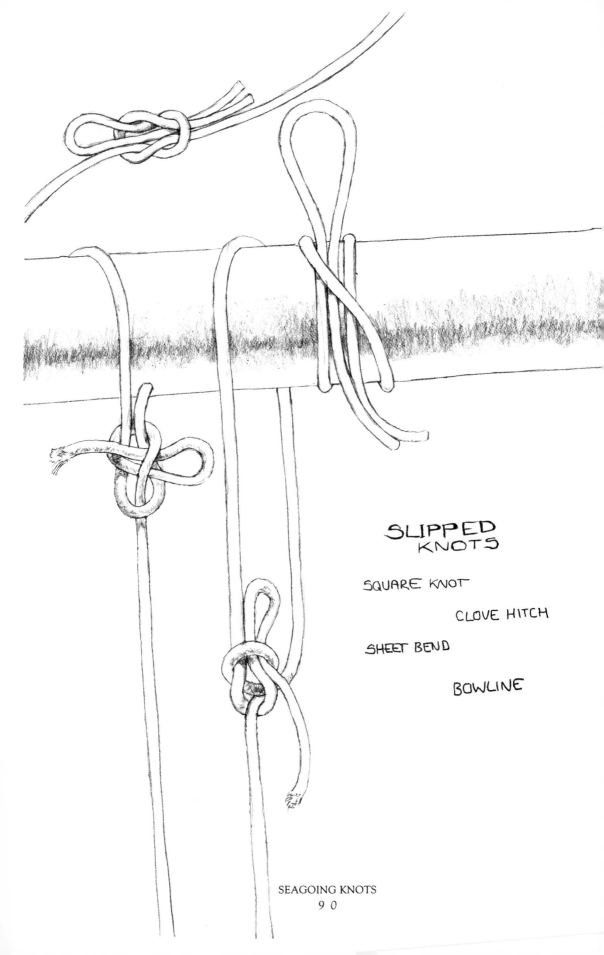

SLIPPED
KNOTS

SQUARE KNOT

CLOVE HITCH

SHEET BEND

BOWLINE

To make a fast release possible when tied to a buoy near a lee shore—or a pricey marina berth—try the slipped half hitch if you are tied to a rail or a ring and a slippery hitch if you are using lines fixed ashore and can belay to your own cleat.

The slipped half hitch shown in the drawing should have the loop worked up to the top of the object around which the knot is taken (far right). It is then more likely to stay put than if left as in the middle drawing. And as with any slip knot, it needs to be snugged up carefully.

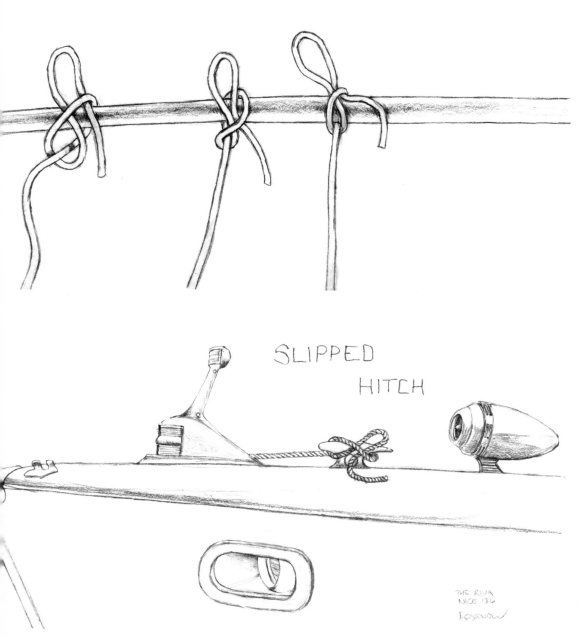

SLIPPED HITCH

THE RIVA
NICE '86
ROSENOW

For slightly better security, you may try the highwayman's cutaway. After working up the bight as seen to the left in the drawing, double the end and put it through the first bight. Snug up to finish.

A jerk at the end, and your nag can be off like the wind.

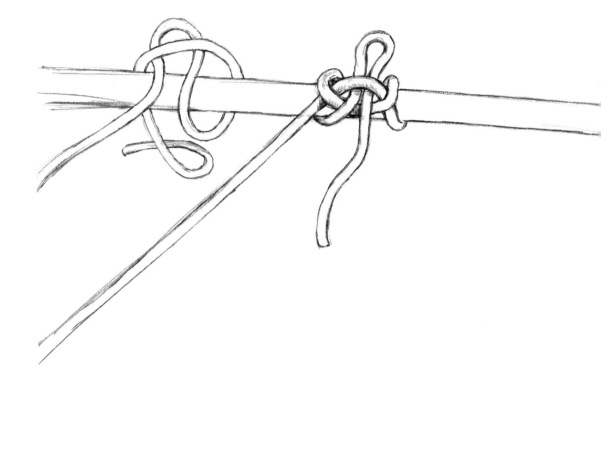

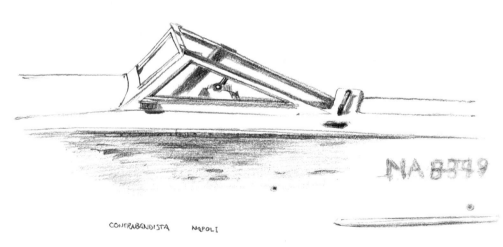

CONTRABANDISTA   NAPOLI

KNOTS IN SPECIAL
MATERIALS

The geometry of a knot must be balanced off against the line it is tied in. On a basic level, this is best recognized in knots made with natural, unprocessed line.

In *Scouting For Boys* (1926), Sir Robert S. Baden-Powell, Bt., gives a "withe knot" along with this description:

"We had no rope with us in West Africa, so we used the strong creeping plants, and also used thin withes or long whippy sticks which we made still more pliant or bendable by holding one end underfoot and twisting the other round and round with our hands. The best wood for withes in England is willow or hazel. You see them used for binding faggots of wood together. You cannot tie all knots with them, as with rope, but you can generally make a timber hitch, or this withe knot."

BADEN-POWELL'S WITHE KNOT

The chief scout makes the point that certain trees (willow and hazel) make better knot tying "line" than others, yet says that all knots can be tied in rope. But as rope differs in its makeup as much as different trees do, there is a great difference in the kind of knot you would use to fasten a cord or a hawser. Making one half hitch in a hawser is quite an achievement, and often sufficient as a mooring if the end is stopped to the standing part.

Old-fashioned knots suitable for straw and suchlike flat materials may now be used to secure webbing ties which are enjoying increasing popularity in marine applications and moorings.

I have used webbing for many years in strops to shorten mainsheet tackles and kicking straps, as well as for permanent docking lines.

WATER KNOT

WEBBING
BEND

KEEP ENDS IN PLACE

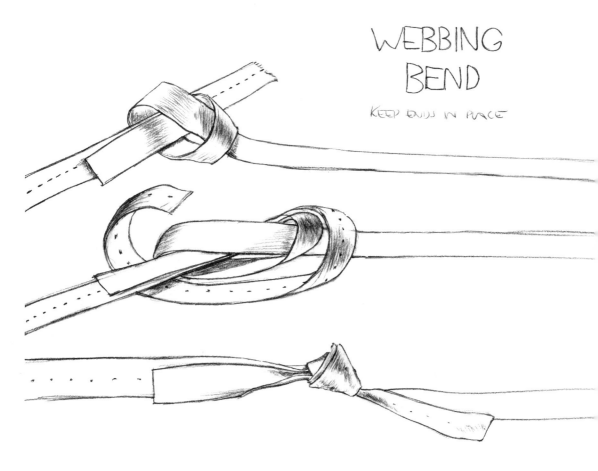

(Obviously, for the mainsheet strop a low-stretch polyester webbing is called for, while a mooring or anchor line application calls for the stretch of nylon webbing.)

To join webbing, use either the webbing bend or the grass knot.

The webbing bend is identical in configuration to the water knot, the name used when the knot is tied in rope. The knot tends to jam in rope but in webbing this quite actually becomes a desirable quality, as it makes for reliability in a tricky material.

To make the webbing bend, simply tie an overhand knot on one end and take the opposite end through the knot in the reverse direction. As with any webbing tie, leave generous tails and pull up the knot forcefully. This will prevent gradual slippage.

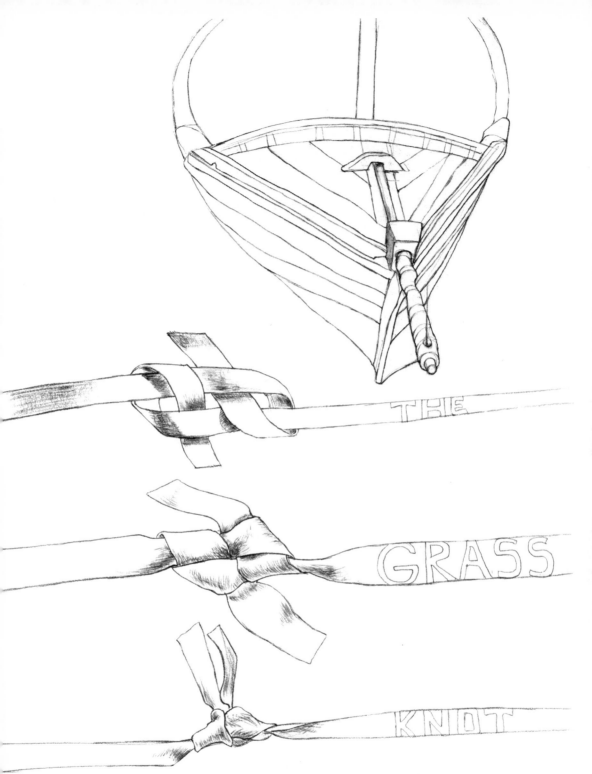

The grass bend, which I last spotted on an Haitian craft rotting away gracefully in the Bahamas, is tied by taking hitches with the ends around opposing standing parts—as drawn here. Under strain, it collapses from an aspect of wickerwork harmony to a tight knob which holds securely but may be hard to unravel.

KNOTS IN SPECIAL MATERIALS

To tie up a ring or horizontal rail using flat webbing, try the latigo knot. Tied as shown, it is constructed like the water knot, holds well and has reasonable resistance to jamming. Make sure you leave a foot-long tail.

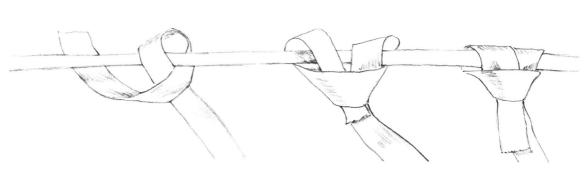

LATIGO KNOT

Shock cord is another tricky material to tie knots in. When I enrolled at the Woollahra Sailing Club on Sydney Harbor as the greenest Australian Moth sailor in the fleet, it was the club Cherub champion who took time out to give some friendly advice on the club lawn. Pointing to his own immaculate arrangements on *Pacific Surfer*, Neville Olliffe said he found a plain reef knot the most satisfactory for joining rope to shock cord.

"I reckon the figure eight knot is the simplest and least slippery for tying clips and such to shock cord . . . pass the cord through the eye of the clip and do a figure eight instead of a half hitch around the standing part."

His advice has since proved very sensible.

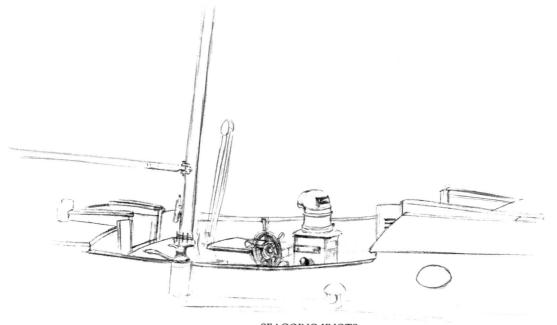

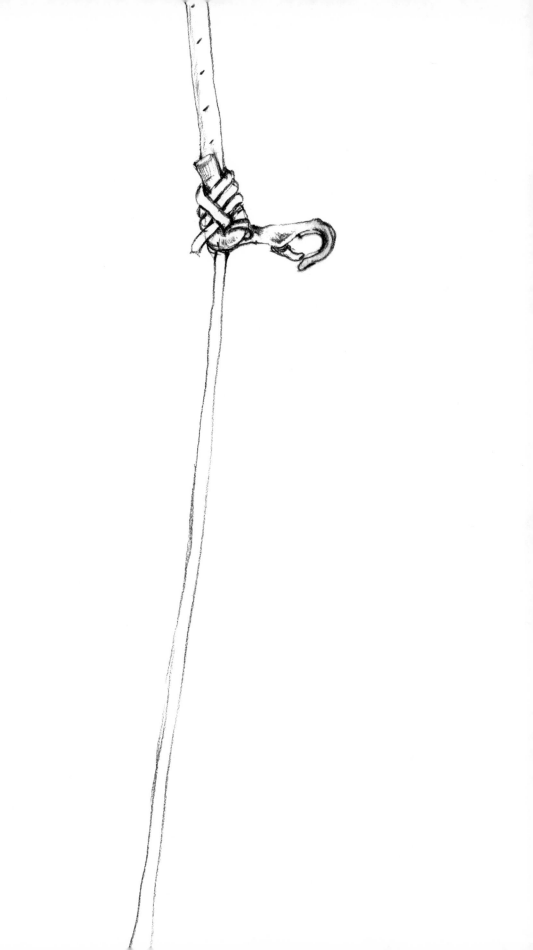

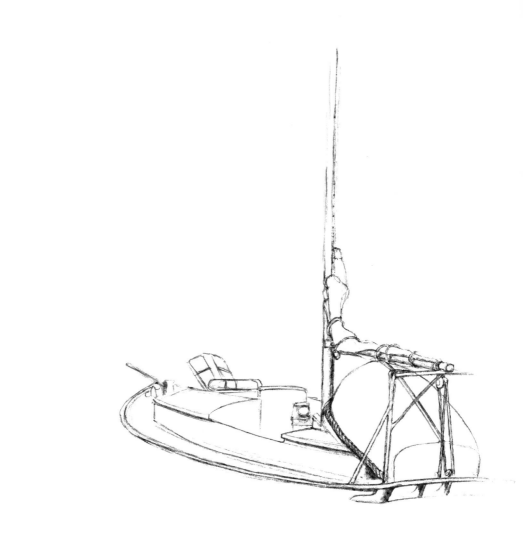

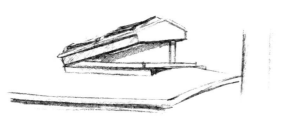

· DAPHNE ·
DINGHY STOWAGE
AND LIFT-OFF
SKYLIGHT ABAFT
MAIN MAST

IN LIEU OF BIBLIOGRAPHY

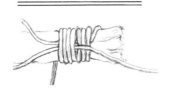

I have tried to share some knots in the sense they became memorable to me. Other writers on cordage have approached the subject in different ways.

The first modern (meaning legible, and fairly comprehensive) work on knots was penned by Dr. Hjalmar August Öhrwall (1851–1929), a professor of physiology at Uppsala University in Sweden. Öhrwall, a follower of the then "radicals" Charles Darwin and John Stuart Mill, had previously written an anonymous guide to contraception (which led to his temporary dismissal from the university) and a work on the tenacity of frogs (*Über die Erstickung und Wieder erweckung des isolierten Froschherzens*, 1887). In his free time, sailing on the east and west coasts of Sweden, Öhrwall concocted *Om Knutar (About Knots)*, which appeared in 1908. Combining scholarship with common sense, the book was later hailed as a trailblazer by the major American knot authors, Ashley and Day.

The first edition was illustrated (an important point this, when it comes to communicate a knot) with the author's photographs of knots. These he suspended on glass in order to eliminate backdrop shadows which would tend to confuse. The photographs were rather small, though, and the second edition (1916) was illustrated with ink line drawings by Öhrwall's daughter Elli. In Sweden, the book has recently been reissued so there may someday be an English translation.

Clifford Warren Ashley (1881–1947), who was born in New Bedford, Massachusetts, and trained with Howard Pyle, was primarily a marine artist but is best remembered for his heavyweight *Ashley's Book of Knots* (New York, 1944). Illustrated with his own charming if sometimes difficult to follow drawings, the work ranges over a vast area and is the most comprehensive knot book we are likely to see for a century or two. Some of Ashley's knots are shown in the context of their proper use, another achievement.

Cyrus Lawrence Day's life (1900–1968) is reminiscent of Öhrwall's in that they were both academicians who are best remembered for their extra-curricular interest in knots. Day was a Harvard Ph.D. specializing in ballads, glees, and catches of by-gone days.

Between indexing such things as "Farewell, my Bonny Witty Pretty Moggy," and "Blowzabella, my bounding doxie," he wrote *Sailor's Knots* (1935) which was later developed into *The Art of Knotting and Splicing* (1947). The latter, by featuring large photographs facing the description of the knot in question, was able to make its points more clearly than Öhrwall and Ashley.

While speaking briefly of writers on cordage and its usage, I cannot leave out the Scots rigger Leonard Popple (?–1966).

In the 1950s, he wrote and illustrated two slim volumes, *Marlinespike Seamanship* and *Advanced Ropeworking*, for Brown, Son & Ferguson, Ltd., in Glasgow.

Though not strictly dealing with knots, these are books on splicing and rope work written straight from the heart. Popple's ink drawings are clear like no other writer's. By concentrating on essential points in the drawings, he easily outdoes even Cyrus Lawrence Day's painstaking photographic illustrations. Popple simply knew—and loved—his cordage.

ABOUT THE AUTHOR
AND ILLUSTRATOR

Frank Rosenow has spent a lifetime with the sea, growing up on a small island, going to sea in his teens, and racing and cruising sailboats all over the world ever since.

As a columnist in *Sail,* he is known for award-winning pencil and watercolor drawings on maritime subjects.

He has trained as a sailmaker in his native Sweden but has practiced little, his love of actual sailing—and drawing—most often seeing him with a foot on the tiller, paintbrush in hand.